THE TWO
CIVIL WAR BATTLES
OF NEWTONIA

THE TWO
CIVIL WAR BATTLES
OF NEWTONIA

LARRY WOOD

THE
History
PRESS

Published by The History Press
Charleston, SC 29403
www.historypress.net

Cover credit: Andy Thomas, artist, Carthage, Missouri.

Images are courtesy of the author unless otherwise noted.

First published 2010
Second printing 2013

Manufactured in the United States

ISBN 978.1.59629.857.6

Library of Congress Cataloging-in-Publication Data

Wood, Larry (Larry E.)
The two Civil War battles of Newtonia : fierce and furious / Larry Wood.
p. cm.
Includes bibliographical references.
ISBN 978-1-59629-857-6
1. Missouri--History--Civil War, 1861-1865--Campaigns. 2. Newtonia (Mo.)--History,
Military--19th century. 3. United States--History--Civil War, 1861-1865--Campaigns. 4.
Missouri--History--Civil War, 1861-1865--Battlefields. 5. United States--History--Civil War,
1861-1865--Battlefields. I. Title.
E473.8.W66 2010
977.8'03--dc22
2010015345

Contents

CONTENTS

Acknowledgements

The research for this book entailed the solicitation and consultation of material from various sources housed at a number of different libraries or other research facilities. I would like to acknowledge the institutions that played a part in my research for this book. They include the Hulston Library at Wilson's Creek National Battlefield, the Joplin Public Library, the Kansas State Historical Society, the Missouri Southern State University Library, the Missouri State Archives, the Neosho-Newton County Library, the Springfield-Greene County Library, the State Historical Society of Missouri, the United States Army Military History Institute, the Western Historical Manuscript Collection–Columbia, and the Western Historical Manuscript Collection–Rolla.

I owe a special debt of gratitude to some of the individuals associated with the facilities mentioned above and would like to mention them by name. Let me start with Jason Sullivan and Patty Crane of the Reference Department at the Joplin Public Library. Thanks for cheerfully fulfilling all the interlibrary loan requests that I submitted. Rilla Scott and Mary Rountree in the Genealogy and Local History Section of the Neosho-Newton County Library provided valuable and able assistance during my several trips to that facility. At the Missouri Southern University Library, archivist Charles Nodler and librarian Gayle O'Neal were very helpful.

I would like to thank the Newtonia Battlefields Protection Association for the help and cooperation that its members provided me during the research and writing of this book, and I especially need to mention several members by name. Kay Hively was an invaluable source of information on the subject of the Newtonia battles for a magazine article I wrote a few years ago and for a brief chapter in a previous book, and she also answered some of my questions for this project. David Weems furnished some information about Newtonia that I did not previously have and also let me use a couple of his photos of the Civil War Cemetery. I would like to thank Tom Higdon for showing me around Newtonia and pointing out landmarks of the two battles when I first started researching this book. I want to thank Larry James doubly, not only for the many images that he graciously let me use to illustrate the book, but also for sharing his vast knowledge of the history of Newtonia, including the two battles.

Another person I want to thank twice is my wife, G.G. She served as the first proofreader of the manuscript and also helped me create the maps and battle diagrams included in the book.

Others whom I would like to mention include J. Dale West, who supplied several images for use in the book, and Bob Banks, who helped me understand the early road system of Newton County and the surrounding area. I particularly need to mention Andy and Dina Thomas, who generously allowed me to use an image of one of Andy's paintings for the front cover of the book.

Lastly, I want to thank History Press editors Jaime Muehl and Laura All. I know that Jaime's thorough and professional edit of the manuscript has made the end product better, and Laura was very helpful in the earlier stages of the book's production.

Introduction

After early successes at Wilson's Creek and Lexington near the beginning of the Civil War, the Confederacy was driven out of Missouri during the winter of 1861–62, and the Union secured the state with its victory at Pea Ridge, Arkansas, in March 1862. The Confederacy's first attempt to reestablish a significant presence in Missouri culminated in the First Battle of Newtonia in late September 1862. The battle was distinguished by large-scale American Indian involvement on both sides. Although the engagement resulted in a Confederate victory, the South could not maintain its presence in the state in the face of overwhelming Union numbers.

Two years later, the Confederacy mounted its most serious attempt to take back Missouri. However, General Sterling Price's ill-fated 1864 incursion into the state ended in bitter defeat, and the final action of the raid, the Second Battle of Newtonia, stands as the last important engagement of the Civil War in Missouri.

The Newtonia Battlefields Protection Association has commissioned three significant studies of the First and Second Newtonia Battlefields. In 1995, Robert Fryman completed an assessment of the sites entitled *Engaged the Enemy Again*. White Star Consulting did an archaeological study in 1998, and Gray and Pape presented a preservation plan in 2000. In addition, the Newtonia Battlefields are currently the focus of a study by the federal government to determine the feasibility of the sites for inclusion in the national park system, either as a branch of the Wilson's Creek National Battlefield Park or as a separate park.

Despite the significance of the battles and the attention the battlefields have received in recent years, no book-length treatment of the actual battles has been published until now. With the approach of the sesquicentennial of America's Civil War, the time is right for a full examination of the First and Second Battles of Newtonia.

Chapter 1

A Neat Village with Tasteful Buildings

Newtonia, 1852–1862

In 1859, Albert Richardson, a newspaper correspondent from New York, took a journey west that included a stagecoach trip from Springfield, Missouri, to Fayetteville, Arkansas. At Cassville, he started on a side trip by horseback to Granby, where he wanted to see the largest and richest lead mining district in the United States. After passing through Gadfly (present-day Corsicana) and stopping at a farmhouse for a drink of water, he continued his horseback ride into Newton County. Describing the next leg of his journey, he said, "In a fertile, flower-covered prairie ten miles wide, an oasis among the hills, I reached Newtonia, a neat village with tasteful buildings."

Richardson's one-sentence description of Newtonia is a testament to the fact that there wasn't much there in 1859. The grassland around Newtonia to which Richardson alluded had been settled during the 1830s and was called Oliver's Prairie after its first white resident, Lunsford Oliver. The site on which Newtonia was later laid out was originally granted to Edmund Dunn in 1840, but there is no evidence that he ever occupied the land. In 1851, Mathew H. Ritchey, a prominent Newton County citizen who had originally settled a few miles to the north at present-day Ritchey, bought the land from Dunn and began building a new home. Completed in 1852, the large, two-story house, often called the Ritchey Mansion, would later

Ritchey Mansion, circa 1910. *Courtesy of Larry James.*

be pressed into service as a military hospital during both Civil War battles at Newtonia.

In 1952, on the one hundredth anniversary of the home's completion, an article about the Ritchey Mansion appeared in the *Neosho Daily Democrat* and contained the following description:

> *Slaves brought from Tennessee molded the bricks and hand whittled the lathe. The doors are sturdy pine slabs and the floors, five brick thick in places, rest upon hewn logs, supported by great slabs of limestone deep underground. The house has five great fireplaces and…two great storage closets that are part of every room. Each room is built to stand as proud and independently as the man who ordered its building. Each room would stand unharmed if all the adjacent rooms were destroyed.*

Built at a cost of $400, the house contained two parlors on the first floor separated by a center hall running north to south and two bedrooms on the second floor that were also separated by a center hall. A first-floor wing of the home off the west parlor served as the dining room, and a separate kitchen was located behind or south of the main house. A stone fence ran

Ritchey barn, circa 1900. *Courtesy of Larry James.*

in front or north of the Ritchey home along the main east–west road (later called Mill Street), and a stone fence also surrounded the three-story stone barn that Ritchey built on his property across the road. The two stone walls formed a lane running in front of and to the west of the house about sixty feet wide and two hundred yards long.

Ritchey laid out the town of Newtonia in 1854, although the plat was not recorded until August 1857. When he laid out the town, Ritchey donated thirteen lots for construction of the Oliver's Prairie Male and Female Academy (later called Newtonia Academy) and an additional parcel of land measuring nineteen by seventeen rods for academy grounds. The street pattern recorded in the original plat showed three north–south streets, later named College, Broadway, and Main, dividing the town into eleven blocks and intersecting Mill Street at the town's southern edge.

Tradition says that Ritchey's wife named Newtonia for a town in the East, although it seems likely that its location in Newton County might have factored into its naming as well. Ritchey helped organize the first business in Newtonia, I.H. Bullard & Company. In 1859, Samuel Cloud became a

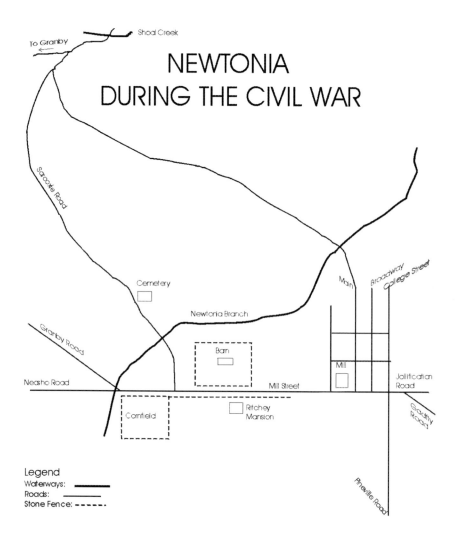

partner in the business, and its name was changed to Samuel P. Cloud and Ritchey. In addition to Cloud and Ritchey, which was engaged in milling and merchandising, Newtonia also had a post office, but there were few, if any, other businesses prior to the Civil War.

At the time of the 1860 census, 240 men, women, and children received their mail through the Newtonia post office, but many of these people lived in the outlying area surrounding the town. By cross-checking the census with land records, Robert J. Fryman, author of a 1995 assessment of the

Mathew Ritchey, circa
1870. *Courtesy of Larry James.*

Newtonia Battlefields, estimated the 1860 population of the town proper at 97 people. This seems consistent with the fact that the 1864 battle map of Newtonia from Cowles's *Official Atlas of the Civil War* shows only eighteen structures in the town at that time.

Politically, the people around Newtonia, like citizens in the rest of Newton County and much of rural Missouri, tended to be what came to be called "conservative Unionists." Many of them had Southern roots, a few held slaves, and almost all of them opposed abolition; yet, the conservative Unionists, including the slaveholders, still supported the Union. Although wealthier than most of his neighbors, Mathew Ritchey, who had been a county judge and a state legislator, was a typical conservative Union man. Despite the fact that he was a native Tennessean and a slaveholder, he was a staunch Union supporter.

With the approach of the Civil War, however, citizens of Missouri became increasingly divided over the issue of secession, especially in many of the state's rural areas, and the region around Newtonia was no exception. To escape the growing partisanship, twenty-two-year-old Mary Grabill, her husband, and her infant son left their Newtonia home on the eve of the war and moved almost two hundred miles to the northeast to Morgan County, Missouri, where they thought the political climate would be calmer.

Looking back at their home territory from a distance, the Grabills must have been glad they had moved away. After hostilities began, General Sterling Price's Southern-allied Missouri State Guard descended on the southwest part of the state to drill and equip its troops in preparation for war. During late July and early August, Newton and surrounding counties were overrun with poorly armed and poorly mounted Southern soldiers seeking to outfit themselves for battle, and according to a correspondent of the *St. Louis Missouri Democrat*, "a fearful state of things" existed in the region. Estimating that most of the horses in Price's army had been "pressed" or stolen "from the counties of Jasper, Barton, Lawrence, and Newton," the reporter suggested that "a general system of outlawry" prevailed and that some of "the wretches in the community" had started taking advantage of the anarchy by preying on their neighbors.

In the fall, after the Southern army had left southwest Missouri, Mrs. Grabill and her family, finding things almost as unsettled in central Missouri as they were back home, decided to return to Newtonia, where, as Mary Grabill said, "we had at least a roof of our own to cover us." The family who had been staying in their home, however, refused to vacate promptly, and the Grabills were forced at first to board at Mathew Ritchey's mansion. Shortly afterward, the store of Samuel P. Cloud and Ritchey closed, and Mary's husband, twenty-nine-year-old E.H. Grabill, went into partnership with Ritchey's twenty-five-year-old son, James M. Ritchey, hauling goods and supplies to Newtonia.

The Grabills' reasoning in returning to Newtonia in the fall of 1861 was that they felt that, since Major General John C. Fremont's Union forces now controlled Springfield, the Southern army was gone for good. They thought things would be settled in the area, and all the fighting would occur farther to the east or south. Years later, Mary would recall in a letter to her daughters, "How we were mistaken in our calculations!"

For a time, things did go smoothly for the Grabills and the rest of Newtonia. Then, in 1862, after Price had been forced out of Missouri, bands of Confederate recruits from northern Missouri began streaming through the Newtonia area, trying to get south to join the Southern army and skirmishing with Union scouting parties along the way. It was during these skirmishes that Mary Grabill first noticed that "Judge Ritchey's big stone barn was always resorted to as a place of safety" by whichever side happened to control Newtonia at the time, and she thought the barn, being a defensive stronghold, was probably the cause of the many encounters in the area.

During the spring and early summer of 1862, no organized military force regularly occupied Newtonia, a condition that meant that the Grabills and other local residents "were subject to prowling bands on either side, who were in the field for revenue only—or revenue and revenge upon former neighbors of the opposing side." The roaming guerrilla bands, Mary Grabill explained, "did not hesitate at any atrocity or act of revenge—for plunder or to get even with an enemy. All manner of cruelty was practiced to extort information about supposedly hidden valuables—horrors too repulsive to tell." Of the two sides, Mary felt the Yankee soldiers were worse pillagers than the Confederates, probably, she conjectured, because, coming primarily from the populated areas where their own families were relatively safe from retaliation, they considered the rural areas enemy territory, whereas the Confederates were drawn mainly from the country and feared revenge on their own families if they committed outrages on others.

By midsummer, Union officials in southwest Missouri had noted Newtonia's strategic location near the Granby lead mines and the importance of holding Newtonia as a deterrent to a Confederate incursion from Arkansas. A semipermanent outpost was established there in July 1862 under Colonel George H. Hall of the Fourth Missouri State Militia Cavalry. In late July, Hall's men were engaged in hauling lead from Granby to Newtonia and on to Springfield, but Hall was shortly afterward ordered to Cassville. Although other officers from other commands occupied Newtonia off and on throughout August and early September, the area continued to be plagued by the prowling bands to which Mary Grabill alluded.

And then, early one morning in late September, Mary and her family were awakened by the boom of cannonading. The skirmishing and plundering in and around Newtonia during the past year was child's play compared to what the Grabills were about to witness.

Chapter 2

The Civil War in Missouri, 1861–1862

The 1860 presidential election was dominated in Missouri by two centrist candidates, Northern Democrat Stephen Douglas and Constitutional Unionist John Bell, each of whom received more votes than the combined total of Republican Abraham Lincoln and Southern Democrat John C. Breckinridge. Lincoln drew most of his support from St. Louis, where the state's fiercely loyal German population was concentrated, while Breckinridge carried a few rural counties, but in general the vote in the individual counties broke along similar lines as the statewide ballot. In Newton County, for instance, Lincoln received only 22 votes and Breckinridge got 255, while Douglas polled 654 and Bell, 406.

The political climate that developed in the state during the days leading up to the Civil War mirrored the results of the recent election. After South Carolina and its sister states from the Deep South left the Union during the winter of 1860–61, a small minority of Missouri's citizens, generally those who had supported Breckinridge, favored immediately joining the seceding states. This group, the Southern Democrats, was disproportionately represented in the state legislature, and it boasted Governor Claiborne Fox Jackson as its most prominent spokesman (even though he had been elected as a Northern or Douglas Democrat). Another small minority, mainly Republicans who had voted for Lincoln, were Unconditional Unionists who supported the Federal government come what may. The leader of this group was U.S. Congressman Frank P. Blair Jr. of St. Louis. By far the largest group, however, was the Conditional Unionists, mostly citizens who had supported Douglas or Bell in the 1860 election. Members of this centrist group pledged to support the Union as long as the Federal army did not try to coerce the seceding states or invade Missouri, and they vowed to oppose any such incursion into their state. Their position was known as "armed neutrality," and their leader was Sterling Price, former governor and Mexican War general.

Despite the Southern Democrats' stronghold in the Missouri legislature, that body agreed to leave the question of secession to delegates elected to a convention for the express purpose of deciding the issue. To the dismay of the secessionists, virtually all the delegates elected to the convention in balloting throughout the state were Conditional Union men, and meeting at Jefferson City in late February, they elected Sterling Price to head the convention. Moving to St. Louis, the delegates passed a resolution in early March 1861 by the overwhelming vote of ninety-eight to one declaring that Missouri should not sever ties with the Union.

After the bombardment of Fort Sumter by Confederate forces on April 12, the chances of Missouri maintaining its position of neutrality faded. On April 15, President Lincoln issued a call for seventy-five thousand volunteers for service in the Union army, and Missouri's quota was set at four regiments. Refusing to comply, Governor Jackson called the requisition "illegal, unconstitutional...inhuman and diabolical," and he declared, "Not a man will the State of Missouri furnish to carry out such an unholy crusade."

Jackson, who earlier had gotten a resolution passed through the legislature condemning any effort of the Federal government to coerce the seceding states, now began organizing Missouri troops for defense of the state and called a special session of the legislature to promote his military plan. Unwilling to wait for official authorization, a company of about two hundred men, mostly from Jackson and Clay Counties, seized the U.S. arsenal at Liberty on April 20 and carried away all the guns and ammunition to help supply the state militia.

Meanwhile, Congressman Blair began recruiting men from the St. Louis area for service in the Federal army, and he secured a company of about eighty men under Captain Nathaniel Lyon to come to St. Louis from Fort Riley, Kansas, to help organize and train the new troops. Tapping the rabid Union spirit of a quasi-military group called the Wide-Awakes that had been drilling in the St. Louis area throughout the spring, Blair had soon enlisted ten regiments, which started training under Captain Lyon.

Although the state legislature was slow to approve the governor's military bill, Jackson, acting under authority already vested in his office, directed the state militia into district camps throughout Missouri. A company of about seven hundred men under General Daniel M. Frost, responding to the order, assembled for training in early May at Camp Jackson (named for the governor), not far from Missouri's other Federal arsenal located in St. Louis. Many of Frost's men had been drawn from a militant secessionist group called the Minutemen, which, like its counterpart, had been drilling in the St. Louis area for weeks. Lyon believed the state troops meant to capture the arsenal, although Frost disavowed such an intention. Prompted by a report that the Missourians had been receiving arms from the South, Lyon decided to act.

With several thousand Federal soldiers, he captured and disarmed the militiamen at Camp Jackson on May 10 and marched them as prisoners back toward the arsenal. Angry, pro-Southern demonstrators gathered and began hurling abuse at the Union troops and pelting them with rocks as they paraded the captives through the streets of St. Louis. Lyon claimed that someone also fired a shot at his men. At any rate, some of the Federals rashly opened fire, and before the mêlée was over, almost thirty civilians lay dead, including two women and a child.

Word of the Camp Jackson affair infuriated secessionists throughout Missouri and drove many Conditional Unionists, including Sterling Price, into Governor Jackson's camp. Had the vote on secession been taken immediately after this incident, there is little doubt that Missouri would have joined the Southern states. The legislature now quickly approved the governor's plan to raise a military force, called the Missouri State Guard, and Price was appointed commander with a rank of major general. A brigadier general was named to head each of nine military districts throughout the state, and James S. Rains, former state senator from Sarcoxie, was placed in charge of the Eighth District, which included the area of southwest Missouri around Newtonia.

Still hoping he could keep the war out of Missouri, Price met in St. Louis with Union general William S. Harney, commander of the West, and negotiated an agreement that Price would preserve order in Missouri and that Federal troops would, in turn, not interfere in state affairs. Blair and Lyon, however, saw the deal as a ruse on the part of Governor Jackson, whom they suspected was merely stalling for time while he trained his soldiers and made arrangements to join the Confederacy. Blair used his influence with President Lincoln to get Harney removed from command and replaced by Lyon, who was appointed a brigadier general.

Jackson and Price sought a conference with the new general with the idea of maintaining the terms of the Price-Harney agreement, and a meeting was arranged for June 11 at the Planters' House in St. Louis. There Jackson and Price offered to disband the Missouri State Guard and try to keep peace in the state if Lyon would disband Missouri's U.S. volunteers, but the fiery Lyon was in no mood for conciliation. He felt that a Union presence in Missouri was mandatory to protect loyal citizens, and after several heated hours of discussion, he declared that it would be better that every man, woman, and child in Missouri should die rather than have the state dictate to the U.S. government. "This mean war," he added as he turned and strode from the room.

Stunned by Lyon's declaration of war, Jackson and Price, after being escorted beyond the Union lines in St. Louis by a Federal envoy, started back to Jefferson City, cutting telegraph wires and burning the bridges over the Gasconade and Osage Rivers along the way to retard a possible pursuit by the Federals. The next day, Jackson issued a proclamation to the people of Missouri condemning Lyon, Blair, and the U.S. government and calling for fifty thousand volunteers to defend the state from Federal aggression. Ordering the commanders of the state guard to concentrate their men at Boonville and Lexington, Jackson then abandoned the state capital. He and a contingent of the militia moved the seat of state government to Boonville, while Price and the rest of the state forces gathered at Lexington.

Meanwhile, Lyon dispatched three regiments under colonels Franz Sigel, Frederick Soloman, and B. Gratz Brown to southwest Missouri to secure that region and to intercept a possible retreat of the state forces in that direction, while he himself started up the Missouri River by steamboat toward Jefferson City with his remaining force, about two thousand men. Disembarking at Jefferson City, he secured the capital for the Union and then continued upriver.

At Boonville on the morning of June 17, he caught up with Jackson and about fifteen hundred state troops under the command of the governor's nephew, John S. Marmaduke. When the fighting began and Lyon brought up his artillery, the undisciplined and poorly trained state troops retreated so rapidly in the face of the booming cannons that the skirmish was later dubbed the "Boonville Races."

Governor Jackson retreated south as Lyon occupied Boonville, and shortly afterward, Price's portion of the state guard abandoned Lexington and also headed south. Leaving General Rains in command, Price went ahead to scout out southwest Missouri for a suitable place to train and equip his new army and to seek the help of General Ben McCulloch, whose Confederate troops occupied northwest Arkansas. In late June, the separate columns under Jackson and Rains reunited at Lamar, where additional troops were mustered into the budding state force before the march south resumed a week later.

The Union soldiers that Lyon had dispatched from St. Louis to southwest Missouri reached Springfield on June 24, and upon learning of the possible joining of the Missouri State Guard and McCulloch's Confederate forces, Colonel Sigel, a veteran of the German insurrection of 1848, determined to cut off such a juncture. He marched to Sarcoxie in late June with about eleven hundred soldiers and intercepted Jackson's state troops, over five thousand strong, on the morning of July 5 north of Carthage. Although many of the recruits under Jackson were poorly mounted and poorly armed, their sheer numbers forced Sigel to retreat to Sarcoxie after a running battle that lasted all day.

Rejoining his troops at Carthage just in time to participate in the victory celebration, General Price then marched them south to Cowskin Prairie in McDonald County, the site he had preselected to train the raw soldiers. With Sigel returning to Springfield, the southwest corner of Missouri was left in possession of the Southern forces, and Price used the next few weeks to drill and equip his army. The Missouri State Guard's occupation of the region was an unwelcome prospect to many citizens, at least to Union observers

CIVIL WAR IN MISSOURI
1861-1862

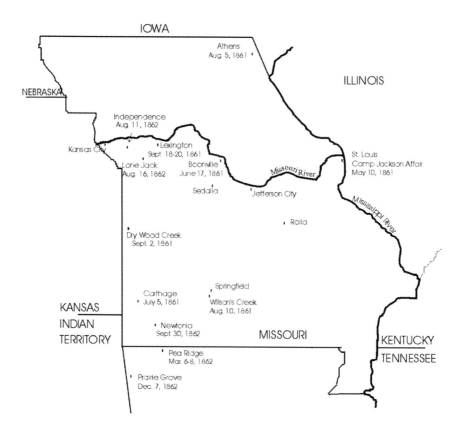

like the *St. Louis Democrat* correspondent who complained, as noted in the previous chapter, that the "pressing" of horses and supplies from area residents by Price's men amounted to a "general system of outlawry."

After three weeks of drills, Price marched his five-thousand-man Missouri State Guard to Cassville in late July. Coming up from Arkansas, McCulloch joined him on the twenty-ninth with over three thousand Confederate soldiers, and about twenty-five hundred Arkansas state troops under General N. Bart Pearce arrived shortly afterward, making a total of almost eleven thousand men. About the first of August, the aggregate force started toward Springfield, where General Lyon, having arrived from northern Missouri after being delayed by heavy rains, was quartered with fewer than six thousand men.

After some minor skirmishing in early August between the advance guards of the two sides, they met in earnest at Wilson's Creek or Oak Hills, about ten miles southwest of Springfield, on the tenth of the month. Each side sustained heavy casualties in the fierce fighting that raged all morning, but after Lyon was killed at about eleven o'clock, the Union forces were soon in full retreat toward Springfield.

The Federals continued their withdrawal to Rolla, but Price did not follow up on the Southern victory, at least partly because the Confederate and Arkansas forces declined to join the pursuit. Instead, Price contented himself with occupying Springfield while McCulloch and Pearce returned to Arkansas.

After a brief stay in Springfield, during which many new recruits flocked to the Missouri State Guard, Price started north on August 25 with an aim of breaking the stronghold on the Missouri River that the Federals had established after driving Jackson from the state capital over two months earlier. Along the way, he took a detour toward Fort Scott, Kansas, where Senator Jim Lane was organizing the Kansas Brigade for the Union, and during a skirmish in Vernon County on September 2, called the Battle of Dry Wood Creek, he drove some of Lane's troops out of Missouri before resuming the march north.

Arriving at Lexington in mid-September, Price found a Union force of about three thousand men under Colonel James Mulligan encamped there, while estimates placed the number of Missouri state guardsmen under Price at five times that figure. The Federals entrenched themselves on the grounds of the Masonic College overlooking the Missouri River, but Price cut off their lines of supply and began bombarding them on September 18. After a three-day siege, Mulligan surrendered his thirsty and hungry troops on September 20. With the Union grip on the river broken, more recruits flocked across from the northern part of Missouri to join the state guard, but Price could not sustain his presence on the river because a large Union force under General Fremont had moved back into Springfield, once again threatening to cut the state guard off from the Confederate forces in Arkansas.

Leaving Lexington on September 30, Price marched back to southwest Missouri, where a special session of the legislature called by Governor Jackson was scheduled to meet at Neosho on October 21. Convening at the Masonic Lodge on the courthouse square, Jackson's government in exile passed an ordinance of secession in late October.

Few sober minds, however, considered the meeting at Neosho a legal assembly. It is highly questionable whether a quorum of lawmakers was present, and the state convention had earlier been vested with full authority to decide the issue of secession. In addition, the same state convention had, in July, installed a provisional state government at Jefferson City to replace Jackson's absent one. The secessionist fervor of a few months ago had already started to cool, and the middle political ground staked out by the Conditional Unionists prior to the war was reasserting itself as Conservative Unionism. To the majority of the state's citizens, Jackson's rump government was fast becoming an irrelevant anachronism.

Despite these facts, Price fired off a hundred-gun salute to the new decree, and many of the soldiers in the state guard got drunk celebrating it. The Confederate government readily approved the ordinance, and many Southern-leaning citizens of Missouri now considered themselves part of the Confederacy.

After the ordinance of secession, the Missouri State Guard accompanied Jackson to Cassville, where he briefly reconvened his government, and then in November, Price established his camp at Osceola. About the same time, the Federal forces at Springfield were ordered back to the railheads at Rolla and Sedalia after General David Hunter replaced General Fremont as commander of the Union's Department of the West. In late December, Price moved into the abandoned city with plans to winter there.

The state guard had scarcely had time to settle in, however, when General Henry Halleck, commanding the newly formed Department of the Missouri, ordered General Samuel R. Curtis to march on Springfield with an army of slightly over ten thousand men. The Union forces reached the outskirts of Springfield in early February and drove Price out of town without a serious fight. Curtis chased the retreating state guard through southwest Missouri and into Arkansas, with occasional skirmishing along the way.

In northeast Arkansas, Price, still pressed by Curtis, linked up with the Confederates under McCulloch, and General Earl Van Dorn, newly appointed commander of the Confederate Trans Mississippi District, arrived on the scene to personally take charge of the combined Southern forces and direct the coming battle. The two sides met in early March 1862 at the Battle of Pea Ridge, also called the Battle of Elkhorn Tavern, in the largest Civil War battle west of the Mississippi. McCulloch was killed during the fighting, and the Confederate forces ultimately retired from the field in defeat.

The Federal victory at Pea Ridge temporarily secured Missouri for the Union, and the Confederacy essentially abandoned the state. Appointed a Confederate general, Price was sent east to reinforce the beleaguered Rebel army in Tennessee, and most of his men followed him into Confederate service. Southern forces would not reenter Missouri in large numbers until six months later in the fall of 1862, when they would once again take up the battle for control of the state at a small town in eastern Newton County called Newtonia.

Chapter 3

American Indian Involvement in the Civil War

O ne of the distinguishing features of the First Battle of Newtonia is the fact that it is one of the few battles, if not the only battle, of the Civil War in which organized units of regimental strength composed of American Indians fought against one another. In some cases, even Indians of the same tribe—in particular, the Cherokees—faced one another on the battlefield at First Newtonia. To fully understand why American Indians of the same tribe ended up fighting on opposite sides during the Civil War, one must go back thirty years or more. Internecine hatreds, predating the 1830s removal of the tribes to Indian Territory (present-day Oklahoma) from the Southeast, were reawakened by the coming of the Civil War, and the old grudges ultimately influenced the decision to align with either the Union or the Confederacy.

A division between the Creek Indians developed when the tribe was forced out of northeastern Georgia in the late 1600s and early 1700s. Tribe members settled farther west and south in separate locations—in western Georgia along the Chattahoochee River and across the border in east central Alabama along the Coosa and Tallapoosa Rivers. Those along the Chattahoochee, who came to be known as the Lower Creeks, had closer contact with white settlers than those in Alabama, who were called the Upper Creeks. The former group slowly began to incorporate white practices, like farming and ownership of private property, and often intermarried with whites, while the Upper Creeks clung to their traditional culture, strongly resisted the encroachment of white civilization, and remained largely a purebred tribe.

In 1812, some of the Upper Creeks decided to strike against American expansionism. Raising a force of several thousand warriors, called Red Sticks because of the red war clubs they carried and the Creek custom of using red sticks to count down the days to the beginning of war, the group started threatening and killing white settlers. The Creek National Council, composed mostly of Lower Creeks, convened to deal with the crisis. The delegates decided that the best way to halt the uprising or at least to distance the Lower Creeks from it was to set an example, and they ordered the execution of Little Warrior, one of the Red Stick chiefs.

In retaliation for Little Warrior's killing, the Red Sticks attacked a Lower Creek town in the summer of 1813, sparking a nine-month-long civil war between the two factions of Creeks. The U.S. government stepped in on the side of the Lower Creeks, and in the spring of 1814, General Andrew Jackson of the West Tennessee Militia attacked a Red Stick camp at Tohopeka, killing about eight hundred warriors, in what became known as the Battle of Horseshoe Bend. Some of the Red Sticks escaped to Florida, but their war for independence was over. After suppressing the revolt, Jackson drew up a treaty calling for the Creek Nation to give up about twenty-three million acres of land to the United States. Leaders on both sides of the Creek Civil War were supposed to sign it, but no Red Stick chiefs could be found.

A series of other treaties obliging the Creeks to cede additional land to the U.S. government followed, including the February 1825 Treaty of Indian Springs, which was promoted by William McIntosh, a chief of the Lower Creeks, whose mother was a Creek woman but whose father was a prominent Scotsman from Savannah. A group of Upper Creeks, led by a young leader and orator named Opothleyahola, went to Indian Springs to oppose the treaty, which called for the Creek Nation to cede the remaining portion of its lands in Georgia. Opothleyahola, who had fought against Jackson at Horseshoe Bend as a young man, gave a stirring speech opposing the treaty, and a majority of the delegates, including some Lower Creeks, repudiated it. That didn't stop McIntosh and a number of his adherents from signing it anyway. Afterward, the Creek Council tried McIntosh under an 1824 tribal law calling for the death of any Creek who ceded tribal land, and a company of one hundred Upper Creeks led by Chief Menawa carried out the death sentence in the spring of 1825.

Opothleyahola journeyed to Washington in January 1826 to protest the terms of the 1825 treaty. He succeeded in getting the McIntosh treaty abrogated, but, bowing to the inevitable, he ended up signing a new treaty in late January containing similar stipulations as the old one. Under terms of the 1826 treaty, the Lower Creeks began voluntarily removing from Georgia to lands west of the Mississippi. The first contingent settled in February 1828 along the banks of the Arkansas River near the mouth of the Verdigris in the newly designated Indian Territory west of Arkansas.

The state of Alabama soon began to agitate for the removal of the Upper Creeks as well, and the tribe was finally cajoled and pressured into signing an 1832 treaty relinquishing all lands east of the Mississippi in exchange for lands to the west. Most of the Upper Creeks continued to resist expulsion from their homeland, and the first contingent had to be forcibly removed in 1836. The following year, Opothleyahola, now chief of the Upper Creeks, led about eight thousand of his people to Indian Territory, where they settled north of the Canadian River and rarely came into contact, at least at first, with the Lower Creeks who had settled farther north.

The intra-tribal conflict that existed among the Cherokees as the Civil War approached, like that of the Creeks, had its origins in the power struggle and political machinations over removal of the tribe from the Southeast. The Cherokees, perhaps the dominant Indian tribe in America during the colonial period and the early years of the United States, had a long history of contact and cooperation with white people, and many members of the tribe, including John Ross and Major Ridge, had sided with the U.S. government during the Red Stick uprising of 1813 and fought with Andrew Jackson's militia against the Upper Creeks at Horseshoe Bend. By the time Jackson became president and proposed in his first address to Congress in 1829 that all Indians be removed from the Southeast to reservations west of the Mississippi, a rift was already beginning to develop among the Cherokees over the question of how best to deal with the increasing pressure to remove.

Major Ridge, his son John Ridge, and his nephews Stand Watie and Elias Boudinot (Watie's brother) emerged as leaders of what became known as the treaty party. Feeling that removal was inevitable, they urged capitulation as the best course and wanted to negotiate a treaty with the government ceding Cherokee lands in the Southeast for lands in Indian Territory, but their voices were in the minority. John Ross, who had been elected principal chief of the Cherokees in 1828, became the leader of the majority opposing removal. Like the schism among the Creeks, the division among the Cherokees tended to break along racial lines. Most members of the Ridge-Watie-Boudinot faction were mixed-blood Indians, while the anti-treaty party was largely composed of purebred Cherokees. Despite the fact that Ross was seven-eighths Scottish himself, the purebreds readily acceded to his leadership because of his facility with the English language and his skill at negotiating. In fact, Ross may have recognized, like his rivals, the inevitability of removal, but he sought to delay it as long as possible and, in so doing, solidified his support among the purebred Cherokees who resisted removal from their ancestral lands.

Pressure for removal of the Cherokees mounted during the early 1830s as other tribes, like the Choctaws, began to remove, and the Georgia Land Lottery was held to distribute Cherokee lands to white citizens. Despite the fact that the Cherokees still occupied the lands, and despite charges of irregularity in the way the drawing was conducted, white settlers began streaming into the Cherokee Nation demanding to take up residence in their new land.

The rift between the Ridge faction and the Ross faction widened as the pressure to remove increased, and the two sides started sending separate delegations to Washington to present their respective proposals to the federal government. Like many contentious debates, one of the key points of dispute involved money. The pro-removal party favored distribution of the annuities promised by the government to the individual members of the tribe, while leaders of the Ross faction wanted the money to go to the general treasury of the Cherokee Nation. The leaders of the Ridge faction accused Ross of plotting to use the money for his own benefit.

During the midst of the contention, in December 1835, John Schermerhorn, President Jackson's commissioner to the Cherokees, called a meeting at New Echota, Georgia, to draw up a removal treaty. Ross refused to attend the meeting and instead sent a delegation to Washington to negotiate a different treaty, and he called on his followers to stay away from the New Echota meeting. However, a majority of those who did attend, mostly members of the Ridge faction, reached an agreement with Schermerhorn, and a committee of twenty, including Major Ridge and Elias Boudinot, signed the New Echota Treaty. John Ridge and Stand Watie, who had been among those dispatched to Washington by Ross, left that delegation when they learned of the New Echota Treaty and added their names to the document as well.

The final version of the treaty was signed by Major Ridge, John Ridge, Elias Boudinot, and Stand Watie, and, over opposition from the Ross delegation, it was ratified in the U.S. Senate in May 1836 by a one-vote margin. After signing the document, John Ridge is reported to have declared that he might not die tomorrow, but sooner or later he would have to give up his life as a penalty for signing the treaty. His prediction would prove prophetic.

In the spring of 1837, Major Ridge and Stand Watie led a small party of Cherokees west to Indian Territory, where a group of fellow tribesmen, known as Old Settlers, were already living. The latter group had migrated from the Southeast to Arkansas years earlier, removed to Indian Territory in 1828, and settled in the three forks area of the Arkansas, Grand, and Verdigris Rivers, while Ridge and Watie settled on Honey Creek just across the state line from present-day Southwest City, Missouri. John Ridge, Elias Boudinot, and other members of the pro-removal faction joined the Watie group later the same year, but most of the Ross party continued to resist migration. During the following year of 1838, the remaining Cherokees, numbering about eight thousand, were forcibly removed, and their arduous journey, during which about half of them perished from hardships encountered along the way, became infamously known as the Trail of Tears. The hardships endured by the anti-removal Cherokees further embittered them toward the treaty party, whose trip the previous year had been relatively trouble free.

The treaty party adopted the government already established in Indian Territory by the Old Settlers, but the Ross faction insisted on the government of the Cherokee Nation East that they had brought with them. A meeting near the Grand River was called in June 1839 to try to reconcile the two forms of government, but members of the treaty party were forced to flee because

Monument to Stand Watie at Ridge-Watie Cemetery near the Missouri-Oklahoma border.

of threats on their lives. After the meeting, a group of tribal members who were especially bitter over the New Echota Treaty met secretly and invoked a "blood law" calling for the execution of those who had signed away their former lands.

The death sentences were carried out on Elias Boudinot, John Ridge, and Major Ridge on June 22, while Stand Watie escaped an attempt on his life the same day. Watie armed a group of his supporters and went about the countryside vainly searching for the killers. The animosity between the Watie faction and the Ross faction that had long smoldered beneath the surface had exploded into violence and now threatened to erupt into civil war. The outnumbered treaty party turned to Washington for protection, and only the threatened intervention of the federal government and alliance with the Old Settlers saved the Watie faction from likely annihilation.

Tension between the treaty party and the Ross faction barely abated, and sporadic violence continued to break out. In 1842, Watie partially avenged the murders of his brother and the Ridges when he killed James Foreman, who had been accused of participating in the assassination of Major Ridge. Watie killed Foreman in a fight at a grocery store located a couple of miles across the border in Arkansas. Tried in the Circuit Court of Benton County, Arkansas, he was acquitted on the grounds of self-defense.

Then, in late 1845, the animosity between the warring factions erupted into another bloodbath. Several killings were blamed on the notorious Starr family, who were treaty supporters, and James Starr and Stand Watie's brother, Thomas, were killed in retaliation. Once again, Stand Watie began to gather and arm his supporters, but a treaty signed the following year by all three groups—the Old Settlers, the Watie faction, and the supporters of Chief Ross—headed off another civil war. Indian Territory then settled into a period of relative calm during the late 1840s and the 1850s.

The old wounds still festered, and the approach of the Civil War once again divided the Indians into rival camps. In 1859, Ross's followers revived an old tribal organization named Kee-too-wah that had vehemently opposed the signing of the Treaty of New Echota. Commonly called the Pins because of the pins they wore on their clothes as badges, the mostly purebred Cherokee group tended not to own slaves and generally favored abolition, although Ross himself was a slaveholder. Meanwhile, the slaveholding Watie and his mixed-race followers became active in the Knights of the Golden Circle, a secret organization that strongly opposed abolition.

Similarly, the coming of the war revived the schism between the Creeks. The Upper Creeks, still following their old chief, Opothleyahola, mostly supported the Union, despite the fact that a good number of them were slaveholders, while the Lower Creeks, now led by Daniel and Chitty McIntosh, sons of the chief who had been slain in 1825 by men aligned with Opothleyahola, tended to favor secession.

At the very outset of the war, the Confederacy, seeing a need to control the land occupied by the Indians, commissioned General Ben McCulloch with three regiments from Arkansas, Texas, and Louisiana to take charge of the military district encompassing Indian Territory. Albert Pike, a successful Arkansas attorney who had represented the Creek Nation and the Choctaw and Chickasaw tribes in separate court cases a few years earlier, was appointed special commissioner to the Indians, and he began trying to enlist the tribes to the Southern cause.

Most of the white agents in Indian Territory favored the South, and they, too, tried to use their influence to line up support for the Confederacy. In May 1861, Confederate secretary of war Leroy P. Walker wrote to Douglas H. Cooper, agent to the Choctaws and Chickasaws, commissioning him to raise a regiment between the two tribes. A native Southerner who had been a Mississippi state legislator and had served with Confederate president Jefferson Davis in the Mexican War, Cooper had little trouble recruiting the Choctaws and Chickasaws, whose lands lay in the southern part of Indian Territory near Texas, to the Confederate side. He soon raised a regiment called the First Choctaw and Chickasaw Mounted Rifles and was made a colonel.

On July 10, near present-day Eufala, Pike negotiated a treaty with the Creeks over the objection of Opothleyahola, who urged neutrality and refused to join the McIntosh faction of Lower Creeks in its pact with the Confederacy. Forced now to choose sides, Opothleyahola declared his loyalty to the Union and began mobilizing his supporters among the Upper Creeks. On July 12, Pike signed a treaty making the Confederacy's alliance with the Choctaw and Chickasaw tribes official. Then, on August 1, he inked an agreement with the Seminoles, although they, like the Creeks, were divided over the issue, and a small band of loyal Seminoles joined Opothleyahola's gathering, along with a scattering of other Indians who rejected their tribes' treaties with the South.

Like Opothleyahola, Chief Ross balked at an alliance with the Confederacy, but in July 1861, Stand Watie, a staunch supporter of the Southern cause, was commissioned a colonel and began raising a regiment, called the First Cherokee Mounted Volunteers, for the Rebel army. While Watie's command was still being organized, a portion of his men fought with McCulloch and General Sterling Price at Wilson's Creek on August 10, 1861, and the Confederate victory there helped convince Ross to side with the South. In late August, he authorized a regiment for the Confederacy under John Drew called the First Cherokee Mounted Rifles, while Watie's command became the Second Cherokee Mounted Rifles. In early October, Ross met with Pike and signed a treaty officially aligning the Cherokee Nation with the South.

After negotiating the treaties, Albert Pike was commissioned a brigadier general in the fall of 1861 and given command of Confederate forces in Indian Territory, but Colonel Cooper assumed command during Pike's November absence and decided to move against Opothleyahola's gathering army, which consisted of several thousand loyal Indians, including an effective fighting force of perhaps one thousand. Cooper marched on Opothleyahola's camp in mid-November with a force of about fourteen hundred men, including his own First Choctaw and Chickasaw Regiment, a Creek regiment under D.N. McIntosh, a Creek and Seminole battalion under Chitty McIntosh and Seminole leader John Jumper, and a detachment of the Ninth Texas Cavalry. The loyal Indians had already abandoned camp and started north seeking sanctuary in Kansas, but Cooper caught up with and attacked them at Round Mountain, west of modern-day Tulsa, on November 19. Although finally forced to retreat, Opothleyahola fought the Confederates on even terms long enough to allow his women, children, and supply wagons to put some distance between themselves and their pursuers.

When Cooper was briefly called back to the Arkansas River, the Federal Indians, rather than continue to Kansas, camped on Bird Creek north of Tulsa, and Cooper, joined by John Drew's First Cherokee Regiment, located them there in early December. After parleying under truce with some of Opothleyahola's warriors, many of Drew's Pin Indians deserted, with some going over to the Federal side, and during the subsequent clash on December 9, usually called the Battle of Chusto Talasah, Opothleyahola once again fought Cooper to a virtual draw, buying time for his forces to retreat.

Cooper then returned to Fort Gibson, where he and Colonel James McIntosh of the Second Arkansas Mounted Rifles planned a coordinated attack on Opothleyahola. When Cooper was delayed, McIntosh declined to wait and attacked the loyal Indians alone on December 26 at the Battle of Chustenahlah in present-day Osage County, northwest of Tulsa, soundly defeating them. Stand Watie and his Second Cherokee Mounted Rifles arrived in time to further rout the retreating Indians under Opothleyahola as they scattered into Kansas.

In March 1862, Pike's Confederate Indians fought at the Battle of Pea Ridge, Arkansas, but his men were criticized for their disorderly fighting during the Southern defeat, and some of them were accused of scalping or otherwise mutilating the enemy dead. Smarting from such criticism, Pike took his troops back to Indian Territory with a vow that that was where they should remain.

Meanwhile, the loyal Indians found refuge in the Neosho River Valley of eastern Kansas, where, during the spring and summer of 1862, they were organized into three regiments composing the Federal Indian Brigade or the Indian Home Guard under Colonel William A. Phillips. When summer gave way to fall, they would meet their fellow tribesmen of the Confederacy on the field of battle at Newtonia to expiate the old wounds that stretched back, in some cases, fifty years or more.

Chapter 4

Prelude to Battle

Summer 1862

During the spring and summer of 1862, after Confederate forces had moved east following their defeat at Pea Ridge, fighting in Missouri, with one or two notable exceptions, was reduced to mere skirmishing. Most of the skirmishing in the southwest corner of the state involved either a remnant of the disintegrating Missouri State Guard under Colonel John T. Coffee, who had balked at Confederate service, or the Indian regiment of Stand Watie, whose mission was to protect the northern section of Indian Territory from a Federal incursion. In fact, on several occasions the state guard and the Indian regiment joined forces to attack Federal camps or skirmish with Union scouting parties.

Watie and Coffee, who had commanded the Sixth Regiment of General Rains's brigade during the early days of the state guard, first hooked up in late April in a chase after two hundred Federals near Neosho. Described by one of his own men as "given to dissipation," Coffee proposed another attack, but he and Watie drank themselves into stupors as they considered the mission. Later, Watie roused and left camp before Coffee could revive enough to resume the powwow.

A month later, on May 31, Coffee and a portion of Watie's regiment again linked up for an attack on a Missouri State Militia Cavalry camp near Neosho. Taken by surprise, the Federals tried to form a line of defense but broke and ran as the Rebels charged. Coffee's mounted troops chased after the fleeing Federals, overtaking and killing about ten of them and leaving the bodies strewn along the road.

Near the end of June 1862, while the Federal Indian Brigade was still being organized, a Union force of about five thousand men, including two Indian regiments, advanced into the Cherokee Nation from Kansas under Colonel William Weer with a mission of restoring the Indian Territory to the loyal Indians who had been driven from it the previous winter. Called the Indian Expedition, the Union force met only scattered resistance at first, mostly from Watie's skirmishers, as General Pike was in the southern part of Indian Territory and declined to meet the invasion.

On July 3 at Locust Grove, a detachment of the Indian Expedition attacked and routed a battalion of Missourians under Colonel J.J. Clarkson, who, over Pike's objection, had been sent into the territory by General Thomas C. Hindman. Still stinging from the criticism his troops had received for their behavior at Pea Ridge, Pike had been involved in a running dispute with Hindman ever since the latter had taken command of the Confederate Trans Mississippi District at the end of May. On July 12, Pike resigned his commission as brigadier general of the Confederate Indians, and Colonel Cooper succeeded to the command.

Meanwhile, a detachment of the Indian Expedition under Captain Harris S. Greeno reached Tahlequah on July 14 and occupied the capital of the Cherokee Nation with no resistance. Many of Colonel John Drew's Pin Indians had already deserted to the Union during the previous ten days, and on July 15, Chief John Ross, in effect, did the same, although Captain Greeno went through the formality of arresting the chief and his immediate followers at Ross's Park Hill home. Taking the Cherokee archives and treasury, Ross was escorted to Kansas under Union guard, and he later went to Washington, D.C., to advocate on behalf of his tribe, staying there throughout the remainder of the war.

While Greeno was at Tahlequah, the main body of the Indian Expedition under Colonel Weer occupied Fort Gibson without opposition on July 15. However, low supplies, oppressive heat, a supposed threat from Confederate forces, and Colonel Weer's "grossly intemperate habits" caused much unrest among the troops. When Weer refused to retreat to a location nearer the

THE INDIAN NATION

Union supply lines, as a war council of his officers urged, Colonel Salomon, his second in command, had him arrested on July 18 and took charge of the expedition. Leaving the two Indian regiments behind as a "corps of observation," Salomon immediately started back toward Kansas with the white troops. Fearing for their safety after having essentially been abandoned, many of the loyal Indians also later returned to Kansas.

A number of former Missouri State Guard officers, such as Captain Joseph "Jo" Shelby, who had gone east with Price after Pea Ridge, returned to the Trans Mississippi during midsummer in 1862 and were sent as Confederate recruiting officers back into Missouri. Here they joined men like Coffee, who, although still clinging to the state guard, had been crisscrossing the state most of the summer gathering men for the ostensible purpose of taking them south. These recruiting efforts and Union attempts to squash them caused much of the skirmishing and guerrilla warfare that characterized the conflict in Missouri during the summer of '62.

On his trip north into Missouri, Shelby and his party, which included Colonel Vard Cockrell and others, approached Newtonia on the afternoon of August 8 and found Major James M. Hubbard of the First Missouri Cavalry holed up on the upper floor of Ritchey's stone barn with two pieces of artillery. The Confederates made a demonstration toward the town that evening, but they quickly fell back and camped outside town when Hubbard opened up with his cannons. After the war, Mary Grabill remembered the occasion as a "bright moonlight night" when she stayed up all night reading a book, unable to sleep because of the booming of the artillery and fear of another attack.

Continuing their trip, Shelby and his party reached northern Missouri in time for Cockrell and Coffee to help lead the Southern charges to victory on August 16 at the Battle of Lone Jack, one of two significant actions to occur in the Jackson County area during the summer of 1862 as a direct result of the Confederate recruiting efforts. Five days earlier, the recruits of Colonel John T. Hughes and Colonel Upton Hays, supplemented by William Quantrill's guerrilla band, had defeated Union forces under Lieutenant Colonel James T. Buel at the Battle of Independence. Although the Missourians were fresh recruits to Confederate service, their victories were not unlikely. Many of them were battle-tested veterans of the Missouri State Guard's early days, and they were well mounted.

After Lone Jack, the triumphant recruits under Hays and Coffee, pressed by a large Union force sent out in pursuit of them, beat a hasty retreat south, while Shelby, who had ventured all the way to his hometown of Waverly on the Missouri River and missed the Battle of Lone Jack, trailed the Federal pursuit. Occasionally skirmishing along the way, the Rebels under Hays,

Coffee, and Shelby finally broke contact with the bluecoats and went into separate camps along the Missouri-Arkansas border.

Meanwhile, Confederate officials in the East, alarmed by Federal inroads into Arkansas since the Battle of Pea Ridge, determined to do something to halt the Union advances. Major General Theophilus H. Holmes was sent west of the Mississippi to take command of the Southern forces there, and the old Trans Mississippi District was restructured as the Trans Mississippi Department. It consisted of three districts, and General Hindman was retained as commander of the District of Arkansas, which included Arkansas, Missouri, and Indian Territory. Hindman was ordered to concentrate most of his forces near Fort Smith and then to push north and try to reestablish a presence in Missouri.

Arriving at Fort Smith on August 24, he found his forces unorganized and the situation in the area less than promising. Hindman's army consisted of about twenty-five hundred infantry, about two thousand cavalry, another fifteen hundred mounted Missouri recruits, and an estimated three thousand Indian troops. His artillery included fourteen guns, but his small arms, in Hindman's words, "scarcely deserved the name." Confederate troops held the line of the Boston Mountains in Arkansas and the line of the Arkansas River in Indian Territory. However, the region of Arkansas and Indian Territory north of Fort Smith was, according to Hindman, "overrun by marauding parties of jayhawkers, tories, and hostile Indians, and was fast becoming depopulated," and the country immediately adjoining the Confederate line was "almost wholly exhausted of subsistence and forage." Farther north, on either side of the Missouri line, was ample subsistence and forage and, just as importantly, "many good mills" for grinding flour and corn.

Pushing forward, the Confederates soon occupied a line roughly corresponding to the southern border of Missouri. Constituting the right flank, a regiment of Arkansas cavalry under Colonel Charles Carroll guarded the road from Carrollton to Springfield. The infantry was concentrated thirty miles to the west at Elkhorn Tavern under command of Brigadier General Rains, who, although still a nominal member of the Missouri State Guard, had been accepted into Confederate service. The Missouri recruits were camped northwest of Elkhorn Tavern near Pineville, and a brigade of Texas cavalry was stationed at Elk Mills, about fifteen miles west of Pineville

NEWTONIA AREA DURING THE CIVIL WAR

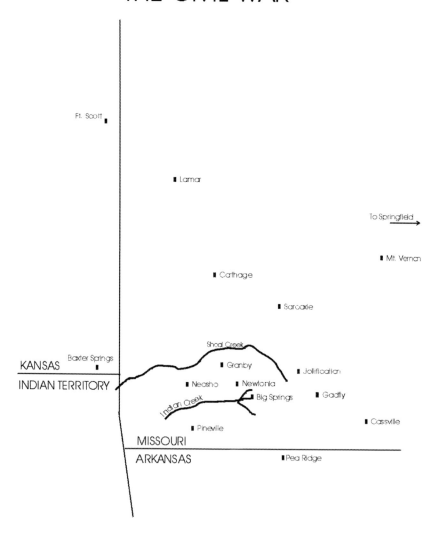

on the Fort Scott road. The Indians, under Colonel Cooper's command, guarded the Confederate left at Carey's Ferry in the Indian Territory, about ten miles west of the Missouri border.

Union officials noted the concentration of forces in southern Missouri under Coffee, Hays, and Shelby almost as soon as they went into camp there in late August, and rumors of a large Confederate force moving up to join them also began to filter north. On August 23, General John M. Schofield, commanding the District of Missouri, wired General Egbert B. Brown, commanding the Southwest Division, suggesting that Brown establish a stronghold west or southwest of Springfield and act in concert on the defensive with Brigadier General James Blunt of the Department of Kansas against the likes of Coffee until Schofield could throw forward enough reinforcements to take the offensive against the larger Confederate force in Arkansas. Brown replied the same day, saying that he had already been in communication with General Blunt and that he (Brown) had suggested Newtonia as the point for such a defensive stronghold.

The next day, General Blunt ordered his division at Fort Scott, comprising three brigades under Salomon (who had been promoted to brigadier general), Colonel Weer, and Colonel William F. Cloud, to move east and south into Missouri, where forage and clean water were abundant. Weer's Second Brigade—consisting of the Tenth Kansas Volunteers, the Tenth Kansas Infantry, the Sixth Kansas Cavalry, the Third Indian Regiment Home Guards, and the First Kansas Battery—marched to Carthage. The Third Indian Home Guard, under Colonel William Phillips, continued to Neosho. Salomon's main force—consisting of the Ninth Wisconsin Infantry, the Second Ohio Cavalry, the Ninth Kansas Cavalry, and two batteries of artillery—remained in the vicinity of Fort Scott. The Second Indian Regiment Home Guards under Colonel John Ritchie, also assigned to Salomon's brigade, moved south to the area of Baxter Springs near the border of Kansas and Indian Territory. Cloud's brigade likewise lingered in the Fort Scott area.

Having established a camp at Big Spring on the headwaters of Indian Creek about six miles southeast of Newtonia, Hays moved up and took possession of the town about the first of September and started running the mill there to supply his men with grain. Phillips sent out a force from Neosho about a week later to drive the Rebels out of Newtonia, and scouting parties under Phillips also skirmished with some of Coffee's men about the same time. However, General Brown's plan for a Union redoubt at Newtonia did not materialize, as Phillips was soon forced to pull back from Neosho in the face of the advancing enemy.

Big Spring area today.

Meeting with Shelby, Hays, and Coffee on September 9 at Elkhorn Creek on the Pineville to Newtonia road, at or near where Coffee had previously established his camp, General Hindman mustered the Missourians into Confederate service and commissioned Shelby as a colonel in command of the brigade. He then ordered Shelby to move north and act as a scout and front guard for the rest of the Confederate troops, particularly the camp of instruction for new recruits that Hindman had established at Elm Springs, Arkansas, about forty miles south of Pineville. Hindman was then called back to Little Rock by General Holmes, and he departed on September 10, leaving General Rains in command of his army.

Shelby moved up to Hays's old camp at Big Spring, now dubbed Camp Coffee, where there was plenty of fresh drinking water. On September 13, a battalion of the First Missouri Cavalry under Captain J.M. Adams marched out from Sarcoxie and briefly took possession of Newtonia, but Shelby came up from Camp Coffee and attacked the Federals the same day. Although Hays was killed by one of the Union pickets at the outset of the skirmish, Shelby's cavalry drove the Federals out of town and several miles across the prairie toward Sarcoxie, once again reclaiming Newtonia for the Confederates.

(Ranging north of Carthage and as far east as Mount Vernon, Shelby's scouts skirmished with Federal detachments on several other occasions over the next two weeks, but the Missouri brigade's headquarters and main force remained at Camp Coffee on the middle fork of Indian Creek.)

A Mrs. Shaw, the wife of a captain in Price's army, was living in Newtonia at the time Colonel Hays was killed, and, anxious to make sure he had suitable burial clothes, she beseeched Mary Grabill to accompany her as she delivered the clothes to Shelby's camp below town. Although Mary came from a Southern family and had relatives fighting for the Confederacy, it was well known that her husband was in the Union army at Springfield, and she was afraid she might be taken captive if she accompanied her friend. Putting aside her fears, she rode in a buggy with Mrs. Shaw "down into the Indian Creek woods," where they witnessed the burial of the "properly clad soldier" in his forest grave and then returned safe and sound to Newtonia.

On September 13, the same day Shelby's forces took possession of Newtonia, General Blunt sent General Salomon into southwest Missouri, by way of Lamar, to support Colonel Weer, and he ordered Colonel Cloud's brigade to the area of Baxter Springs with orders to support Weer and Salomon if they required assistance but otherwise to clear out the Indian Territory below Baxter Springs and hold it. Colonel Ritchie's regiment of Indian Home Guards, previously in the Baxter Springs area, moved into Missouri northwest of Carthage.

Falling back to Mount Vernon after his skirmish with Shelby's cavalry, Captain Adams reported that the Confederate force at Newtonia was much larger than his own. General Brown, now commanding Union troops in the field at Mount Vernon, reported to General James Totten, who had replaced Brown at Springfield, that "the enemy at Newtonia formed in a line of battle, and, when threatened by our cavalry, formed into squares and marched considerable distance in that formation, showing that they are well drilled and organized troops."

General Totten sent dispatches to General Blunt, General Salomon, and Colonel Weer requesting the cooperation of General Salomon and Colonel Weer with Brown's troops at Mount Vernon and suggesting that the Kansas brigades occupy Sarcoxie to intercept a possible Confederate movement toward Springfield. Complying in part with Totten's request, General Blunt sent Salomon to Sarcoxie, but he ordered Weer, who had already marched to Mount Vernon to reinforce Brown, to move back west toward Neosho. In his reply to Totten on September 17, Blunt assured the general that the requested help was on its way to Sarcoxie but suggested that he felt, because Union forces were not yet concentrated and some of them not even properly armed, that the best policy would be "to bluff them by bold dashes against their lines and hold them in check until we have our force all in hands; then we can make a combined offensive movement against them."

Salomon arrived at Sarcoxie on the morning of September 22, while Weer, moving farther west as ordered, camped on Jenkins Creek a couple of days later about five miles from Sarcoxie. Both were now under orders from Blunt not to comply with directives from General Totten without checking

General James G. Blunt.
Courtesy of J. Dale West.

with Blunt first; nor were they to reinforce Brown unless his troops were directly threatened by a superior force.

Sometime in mid-September, after General Hindman had left for Little Rock, the Texas cavalry brigade and the Confederate Indians combined their forces under Colonel Cooper's command at Scott's Mill, nearer to Pineville than either of their previous camps. Here, Tresevant C. Hawpe's Thirty-fourth Texas Cavalry fell in with a part of Stand Watie's Indian regiment that included Tom Livingston's guerrilla command. Although officially attached to Watie's regiment, Livingston's company, sometimes called the Cherokee Rangers or the Cherokee Spikes, was composed mainly of Missourians from Jasper County and acted as a roving, independent band much of the time, just as Watie's regiment sometimes acted independently of the larger Indian command under Cooper. Veering west into Indian Territory, the combined force of Texans, guerrillas, and Indians marched up the Grand River Valley toward Baxter Springs and trailed Colonel Ritchie's Second Indian Home Guard Regiment into Missouri. Catching up with Ritchie northwest of Carthage on the morning of September 20, the Confederates attacked the Federal Indians at their camp on Spring River at a crossing called Shirley's Ford (which got its name from John Shirley, an early settler in the area, whose daughter, Myra Maybelle Shirley, would go on to become the infamous Belle Starr). The Federal Indians, who had brought along their families for the jaunt into Missouri, were put to flight in the initial attack, and the women and children joined in the stampede. However, Ritchie later mounted a counterattack, and according to his after-action report, the day's fighting ultimately left about twenty men dead on each side.

Although General Hindman had left Rains with instructions to make no aggressive movement unless directly assailed, Rains sent a dispatch to Colonel Cooper on September 23 ordering him to form a junction with Shelby's brigade. Cooper broke camp at Scott's Mill the next morning and marched north along the Pineville Road. A few miles west in Indian Territory, Colonel Watie started up the Grand River Valley toward Kansas at about the same time with his Cherokee regiment.

After passing through Pineville, Cooper reached Camp Coffee on the evening of the twenty-sixth. The following day, as senior officer, he assumed command of the aggregate Confederate force, comprising a provisional division, and he sent Hawpe's cavalry regiment and a Cherokee battalion under J.M. Bryan to occupy Newtonia and to operate the mill there, as he later reported, "for the purpose of supplying the command with breadstuffs."

Hawpe and Bryan reached Newtonia about eleven o'clock on the morning of the twenty-seventh, and Hawpe promptly reported to Colonel Cooper that the village was a suitable place for an outpost. Cooper sent up Captain Joseph Bledsoe's two-gun battery to help secure the town, and Hawpe posted pickets on the roads to Neosho, Granby, and Sarcoxie.

Colonel Weer learned of the concentration of Confederate forces almost as soon as Cooper arrived at Big Spring. From his camp on Jenkins Creek, Weer had sent out two scouting parties, one to Granby and one farther west to Shoup's Mill, and both returned on the night of September 26, reporting similar findings. The Confederates had, as Weer reported to General Salomon, "made a significant movement within the last twenty-four hours." The scouting party to Granby had captured and brought back two prisoners, one a Rebel soldier and the other a private citizen who had previously been in the Southern army, and both confirmed what the scouts had learned from other sources. Cooper had reinforced Shelby below Newtonia with seven regiments of mounted Texans and six artillery pieces. Shelby had an additional two cannons, and the total Confederate force at Newtonia now numbered about ten thousand. Weer felt that this figure was surely exaggerated and placed his own estimate at about four thousand, but he was no less concerned by the enemy movements.

He had also learned that Stand Watie and Livingston were in the vicinity of Baxter Springs, and he fretted that they might be trying to flank his forces so that the Confederates could launch a combined attack from two different directions. At any rate, he felt an attack of some sort was imminent. Tired of waiting for the Federals to attack, Weer reasoned, Cooper had obviously moved up to take the initiative. Weer requested, should the expected attack fall on him, that Salomon reinforce him, and he promised likewise to come to Salomon's aid if the Confederates attacked the general first. Colonel Weer suggested that General Brown at Mount Vernon should be advised of the enemy activity so that he could move to reinforce the Kansas brigades and other high-ranking Union officers in Missouri might be apprised of the situation. In the meantime, Weer would send out two new scouting parties, one in the direction of Newtonia and the other in a westerly direction. He admitted that all of these precautions might prove unnecessary, but Weer was convinced that Cooper's moving up from below Pineville to near Newtonia "certainly means something. My information says it means attack."

Instead of moving to flank the Federals camped on Jenkins Creek as Weer feared, Watie was marching up the Neosho River Valley toward the Osage Mission, located at present-day St. Paul, Kansas. (The Grand River becomes the Neosho River in Kansas.) On September 26, some Osage scouts whom Watie had captured about twenty miles below the mission and turned loose a few hours later reported to General Blunt at Fort Scott that Watie was trying to win the Osages over to the Confederate side and had already succeeded in a few cases. Blunt sent Colonel Cloud's regiment later that evening in the direction of the Osage Mission to try to intercept the Confederate Cherokees.

After receiving Weer's dispatch informing him of the concentration of Confederate forces near Newtonia, Salomon forwarded the intelligence to General Brown late on the night of September 26. Brown replied the next morning promising to "move to the west and make a diversion in your favor" but also emphasizing that he had positive orders "not to bring on any battles or engagements, but to fall back in the direction of Springfield if threatened with an attack by superior forces." He reiterated that he would come to Salomon's aid should Salomon's troops become engaged.

The flurry of messages passing among Union officers continued throughout the day on the twenty-seventh, with Weer and Salomon reporting the situation in the field and the commanding generals back at headquarters maneuvering to meet the Confederate threat.

The scouts Weer had sent out the previous evening were back in camp by noon on the twenty-seventh. The western scout reported "nothing but bushwhackers or scouts," but the southern one went to Granby and found the place occupied by four hundred Confederates who had just arrived from Neosho. The Union scouting party drove in the enemy pickets, killing two and capturing one, the latter dressed in full Federal uniform. The captain in charge of the scouting party told Weer that Shelby, Coffee, and Rains had made a junction and that the total Confederate force numbered about eleven thousand. Although skeptical of the intelligence, Weer promptly relayed it to

Salomon. One thing was certain, he concluded. "The enemy are moving in united force this way."

"They outnumber us," Weer continued. "Some point should be selected, there to stand, and the troops in our rear should come forward by forced marches. If inattention to the warnings that have been sent lead to the sacrifice of our forces, a great crime will rest upon some one's shoulders."

No doubt still stinging from his arrest a couple of months earlier at the hands of Salomon, Weer demanded to know what Salomon proposed to do and what measures should be taken in the event that no reinforcements were brought up from the rear. Finally, he suggested that the information from his scouts should be forwarded to General Brown at Mount Vernon.

A courier carrying Weer's message rode into Salomon's camp later the same day, and Salomon, complying with Weer's request, promptly forwarded the message to Brown. Adding a communication of his own, Salomon acknowledged receipt of Brown's morning dispatch and supplemented Weer's report with his own intelligence. A scouting party he had sent toward Newtonia early in the day had just returned reporting a large Confederate force of up to eight thousand men at the town and camped just south of it. Salomon told Brown that Weer would join him at Sarcoxie later that night and that he also expected Brown to send him reinforcements as soon as possible.

Brown, in fact, had already started his Fourth Brigade Missouri State Militia toward Sarcoxie shortly after his morning dispatch to Salomon, and he had sent a message to General Totten at Springfield reporting the movement of his troops. General Schofield, who had come to Springfield to take charge of Union troops in Southwest Missouri when General Curtis assumed command of the Department of the Missouri on September 24, replied to Brown later on the twenty-seventh approving Brown's disposition of troops for the support of Salomon and Weer. Schofield had just received a dispatch from Curtis to be forwarded to Blunt placing Blunt's Kansas troops subject to his (Schofield's) orders, and he asked Brown to communicate this fact to Salomon and Weer. His instructions to Brown and the two Kansas commanders were to stay within supporting distance of each other and to unite if either were seriously threatened. They should attack, however, only "should a favorable opportunity offer" and should "not on any account risk a defeat. You will regard your commands as forces of observation merely."

Schofield also replied to Curtis on the twenty-seventh to acknowledge receipt of his dispatch to Blunt and to assure him that it would be promptly delivered. Schofield told Curtis that the combined force of Brown and the Kansas troops near Sarcoxie would be about sixty-five hundred and that another division of about seven thousand that was being organized at Springfield under General Totten would be ready to move within two days. Schofield assured Curtis that, after bringing any additional Kansas troops that were available to within supporting distance, he would be able to hold his position or perhaps advance.

When Schofield forwarded General Curtis's dispatch to Blunt on the evening of September 27, he also included a letter of his own asking Blunt to send forward from Fort Scott in the direction of Sarcoxie all the infantry and artillery he could spare. Although the Confederates might have superior numbers, Schofield felt that the Union forces were better prepared. Growing bolder than he had been in previous communications, he boasted that the Federals were ready to do battle if the Confederates would meet them. "Should you determine to take the field in person," Schofield concluded, "I shall be happy to meet you, general, and doubt not that we can soon make Rebels scarce in this part of the country."

By Sunday, September 28, the Union forces were partially consolidated. Weer had joined Salomon at Sarcoxie, and Brown's militia had moved down from Mount Vernon and camped on Center Creek within supporting distance of the Kansas troops. Less than twenty miles away, south of the Shoal Creek woods and across Oliver's Prairie, several thousand Confederates were lying in wait at Newtonia. Which side would attack first?

Chapter 5

The Eve of Battle

September 29, 1862

O n the morning of September 29, General Salomon sent out scouting parties from Sarcoxie to Granby, Neosho, and Newtonia. The scouts to Granby came back and reported no enemy present in the town. When the patrol that went to Neosho, a group that was from Weer's brigade, returned, the scouts reported to the colonel that they had skirmished with Confederate pickets, killing two, wounding several more, and taking one prisoner.

The reconnaissance to Newtonia was led by Lieutenant Colonel Edward Lynde of the Ninth Kansas Cavalry and consisted of four companies of his regiment, totaling about 150 men, and two mountain howitzers. Proceeding cautiously, the patrol had advanced about eight miles along the Newtonia road when it began encountering Confederate pickets and driving them in. With the Southerners falling back without resistance in the face of the Federal advance, Lynde and his patrol pressed on toward Newtonia until they reached a spot on the prairie about a mile and a quarter northwest of town, where Hawpe had posted a strong guard in and around a deserted farmhouse and cornfield east of the road. Glancing around, Lynde saw a second Confederate outpost still farther to his left.

When the Confederate pickets stood their ground as though to contest a further Federal advance, Lynde ordered Captain Charles F. Coleman's company to watch the movements of the pickets while Lynde oversaw the

High ground northwest of Newtonia as it appears today.

disposition of the rest of his force. Lynde directed the mountain howitzers of Lieutenant Henry H. Opdyke to shell the house and cornfield, with a company under Major James M. Pomeroy covering the howitzers and the remaining two companies under Major Edwin P. Bancroft guarding the Federals' right flank. A few rounds from the howitzers sent the Confederate pickets scurrying toward Newtonia and the shelter of stone walls and houses.

Alerted by the boom of the howitzers, Colonel Hawpe sent a messenger galloping toward Camp Coffee to request reinforcements. Cooper immediately ordered a portion of his command, including Shelby's regiment and the regiment of Beal G. Jeans (who had succeeded to the command of Hays's regiment after Hays's death) to get ready to ride. About the same time that Hawpe's runner rode into camp, a scout from Granby also arrived and reported that the town was occupied by a group of Pin Indians and Federals. Knowing the importance of holding the lead mines at Granby, Cooper sent Colonel James G. Stevens and his Twenty-second Texas Cavalry (also called the First Texas Partisan Cavalry) to reconnoiter the place and, if possible, drive the enemy from the town. Cooper then sprang to the saddle himself and, along with Shelby and Jeans, started toward Newtonia to the relief of Hawpe.

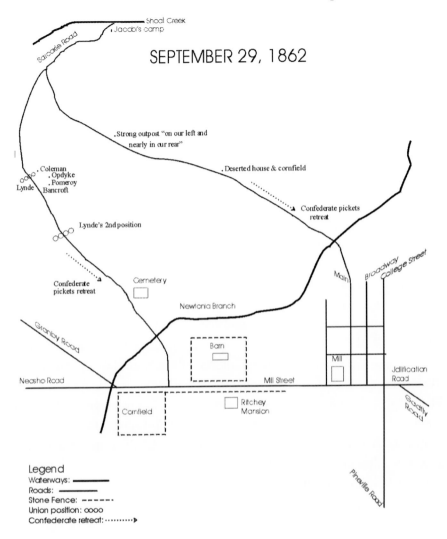

Meanwhile, Lynde crept to within three-quarters of a mile of Newtonia, where Lieutenant Opdyke again opened up with his two mountain howitzers, but Lynde quickly realized he was still too far away from town to do any damage. When the Confederates declined to reply to the cannonading, Lynde sent out patrols and made what other observations he could during the lull. After about an hour and a half, the scouts brought back two prisoners, who told Lynde that Newtonia was occupied by about twenty-six hundred Rebels and two pieces of artillery. Declining to launch an assault against a superior force, Colonel Lynde fell back slowly to the north side of Shoal Creek, where he rested for a while before proceeding toward Sarcoxie.

The Confederate reinforcements reached Newtonia about the same time that Lynde began his retreat, but Colonel Cooper decided not to pursue the Federals. Instead, he stayed in Newtonia throughout most of the day and then, toward evening, returned to Camp Coffee, leaving Shelby and Jeans at Newtonia to reinforce Hawpe.

Hearing the distant echo of the howitzers a few hours after Lynde had left Sarcoxie, General Salomon rightly assumed that the reconnaissance party had run into trouble. He immediately ordered a patrol under Lieutenant Colonel Arthur Jacobi of the Ninth Wisconsin Infantry to ascertain Lynde's whereabouts and reinforce him if necessary or scout the enemy near Newtonia and determine its strength and position and the number of its artillery. Jacobi left Sarcoxie about 3:00 p.m. with two companies of the Ninth Wisconsin totaling one hundred men, three pieces of Captain Job B. Stockton's Twenty-fifth Ohio Volunteer Light Artillery battery under Lieutenant Julius L. Hadley, a forty-five-man detachment of Captain David Mefford's Sixth Kansas Cavalry company, and fifty men of the Third Indian Home Guards.

About three miles from Sarcoxie, Jacobi met Lynde's detachment returning to camp. After consulting with Lynde, Jacobi decided to continue toward Newtonia. Striking a belt of timber near the same spot where he met Lynde, Jacobi sent out scouts on either flank and proceeded carefully. Near dark, he came to Mathew Ritchey's farm about three and half miles north of Newtonia (at the site of present-day Ritchey), where he camped for the night.

When Lynde reached Sarcoxie and reported to Salomon that Jacobi "had taken a position of observation" near Newtonia and wanted reinforcements, Salomon sent two more companies of the Ninth Wisconsin Infantry to support Jacobi, and they reached his camp at Ritchey's farm about eleven o'clock on the night of the twenty-ninth. The officer in charge of the arriving detachment also carried a message that Lynde would join Jacobi in the morning and that their job was "mainly to find out the enemy, but not to risk anything" and immediately report to Salomon if they found the enemy in force.

Chapter 6

The First Battle of Newtonia

Morning, September 30, 1862

Jacobi roused his men early and resumed the march toward Newtonia shortly before daybreak on September 30. He sent out the Third Indian Home Guard as an advance guard and as flankers with instructions to halt and wait for further orders if it found the Confederate pickets. To gain more accurate information as to the lay of the land and the position of the enemy, Jacobi personally led a small scouting party that passed through the timber onto the edge of the prairie a short distance ahead of the advance guard. Discovering the Confederate pickets on a ridge about a mile northwest of Newtonia, Jacobi ordered his command to halt in the timber so as to conceal its strength while he sent out additional scouts to reconnoiter the Rebel position.

The reconnaissance quickly determined that the main body of the Confederate force occupied Newtonia, while a strong picket was posted in a cornfield about a half mile north of the village. (Jacobi said the cornfield was northeast of the village, but it was more likely north, since his own position was northwest rather than due north of Newtonia.) Jacobi sent Captain Mefford and his detachment of the Sixth Kansas Cavalry to proceed in a left flanking movement along the edge of the Newtonia Branch timber to try to cut off the pickets from the main Rebel force. Some of Mefford's men were discovered before they could intercept the picketers, who fled toward

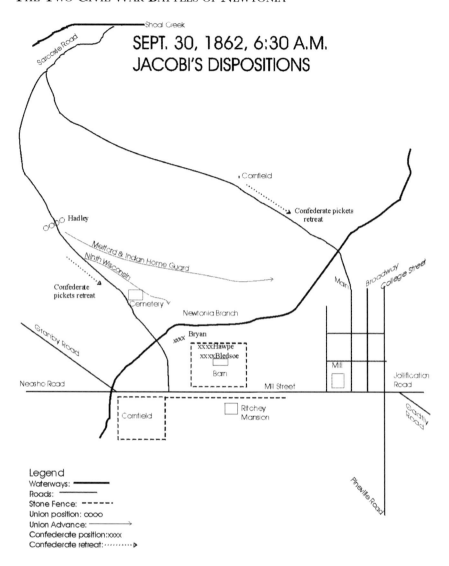

Newtonia with the Kansans in pursuit. With the element of surprise now gone, Jacobi quickly ordered the Indian Home Guards to reinforce Mefford, and he sent the infantry under Captain Gumal Hesse to occupy a wooded ravine north of the village along Newtonia Branch. He ordered the artillery under command of Lieutenant Hadley to take up a position on a swell of land about fifteen hundred yards northwest of town. As soon as the Ohioans reached the high ground and unlimbered their artillery, they opened fire with solid shot at Ritchey's large stone barn, where many of the Confederates were holed up.

Although Colonel Hawpe had sent out heavy scouts on the night of the twenty-eighth, he apparently sent none out on the night of the twenty-ninth, or else they were confined to the immediate vicinity of Newtonia, because just after daylight on the morning of the thirtieth, Shelby and Jeans returned to Camp Coffee with their regiments. Having received no report of Federals in the neighborhood, Hawpe sent a message to Colonel Cooper that no enemy was advancing on the outpost at Newtonia.

Less than half an hour later, gunfire north of town disturbed the morning calm, and Hawpe's pickets came charging into Newtonia. No doubt embarrassed by his serious miscalculation, Hawpe immediately sent a courier racing toward Camp Coffee with word that he was under attack. He then dismounted his Thirty-first Texas Cavalry and formed its men inside the stone fence surrounding the Ritchey barn. He ordered Bryan's battalion to dismount and take up a concealed position in the brush along the low ground about fifty yards in front of the Texans, and Bledsoe's battery he placed inside the stone wall alongside his own regiment. Hawpe had just gotten his five hundred men in position when Hadley's artillery opened fire. Bledsoe's cannoneers immediately replied, sending six-pound solid shot hurtling toward the Union position. It was not yet 7:00 a.m., and the battle had been joined.

After a few hours' rest back at the Sarcoxie camp, Colonel Lynde sounded a "call to horse" during the wee hours of the morning on the thirtieth and started back toward Newtonia at 3:00 a.m. with the same command he had led the previous day. When he reached Newtonia shortly before seven o'clock, he found that "the action had already commenced." Mefford's cavalry detachment had driven in the pickets, the infantry had already been ordered forward by Jacobi, and Hadley had fired three rounds from each of his big guns.

Lynde took charge of the Union forces and ordered the artillery forward about five hundred yards in the direction of the stone barn. Extending the Federal line to the right of Hadley's cannons, he sent the Ninth Kansas Cavalry under Majors Bancroft and Pomeroy, along with Lieutenant Opdyke's two howitzers, to the high ground northwest of town, and he directed Captain

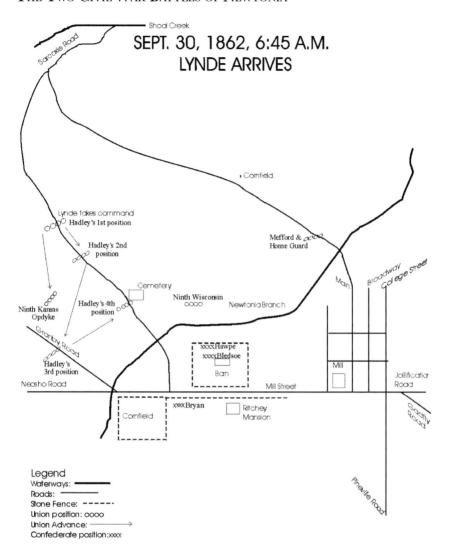

Mefford to occupy the Union left. As soon as the cannoneers unlimbered and got their guns in place at their new locations, according to Lynde, "The artillery opened on the town in gallant style with shot and shell."

Despite the Union's "gallant" display, the Confederate cannoneers seemed to be getting the better of the artillery duel at first. After firing several rounds from his new location, Hadley decided that the position was "unfavorable to effect much," and he asked permission to move to a point about a thousand yards west on a slope overlooking the town. Since Bledsoe's artillerists had, in Lynde's words, "got the range of our guns," the colonel readily granted the request.

Unlimbering his three-inch rifles on the eminence west of Newtonia, Hadley resumed his bombardment of the Confederate position near the Ritchey barn, while Bledsoe's gunners replied with "a brisk and well-directed fire from the town of solid six-pounder shot and twelve-pounder spherical case." The artillery duel raged for almost an hour, with Hadley firing twenty-five rounds of solid shot from each of his three guns. When the Union barrage failed to silence Bledsoe's guns, Hadley finally decided that the Confederate battery was too well covered for him to do much damage from his current position and that his own men were too exposed.

Marching by his left flank, he advanced toward the front until he achieved the cover of brush and low ground northwest of town and then proceeded to within six hundred yards of the Ritchey barn. As soon as the Union gunners were in position, they switched from solid shot to canister and opened fire. "The artillery," according to Lynde, "now played on the position of the enemy with marked effect, dealing death and destruction at each discharge." Under cover of the Federal cannonade, Jacobi's infantry also pressed forward.

Having received word from Hawpe early on the morning of the thirtieth that no Federals were in the vicinity, Colonel Cooper turned his attention to more mundane concerns like taking possession of and holding the area's valuable lead mines, and he ordered Colonel A.M. Alexander's Thirty-fourth Texas Cavalry to proceed to Granby and relieve Colonel Stevens. Leaving Colonel Shelby in command at Camp Coffee, Cooper joined Alexander at the head of the column as the march began shortly after daylight. The regiment had ridden only a couple of miles in the direction of Newtonia when the men "saw the smoke and heard the report of artillery." Cooper ordered the Texans to put their horses to a gallop.

Arriving at Newtonia, Cooper "found our force hotly pressed by superior numbers of the enemy." Cooper directed Alexander to take up a position on the Confederate right, below Ritchey's mill along the creek, and the Texans, dismounting when they reached the designated spot, promptly carried out the order "under a strong fire of grape and Minie balls."

The artillery fire that greeted the Texans was the work of the Ohio cannoneers. Alexander's men had scarcely taken up their position before

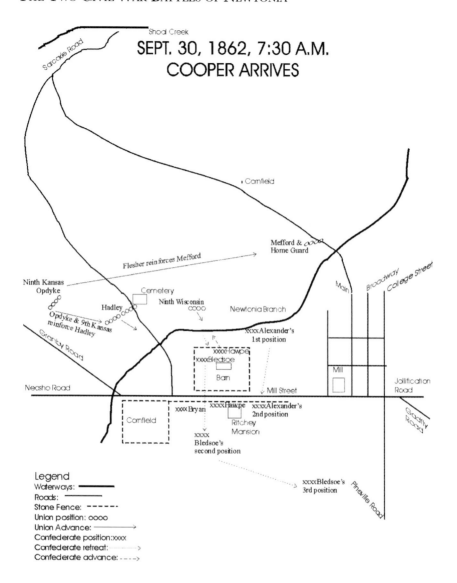

Hadley spotted them in the ravine along the branch three hundred yards to his left front, and the Federal guns opened fire with canister, quickly "driving them into town," according to Hadley, "with severe loss on their side."

Hadley then turned his left piece to the stone wall east of the barn, which was lined with Hawpe's cavalry, while his two right guns engaged Bledsoe's artillery on the west side of the barn. By now, the Federal infantry had gained possession of some of the buildings at the edge of the village, and their sharpshooters were starting to pick off the Confederate artillerymen standing beside their guns. Forced to drop back, Bledsoe's battery took up a new position about three hundred yards to the rear of the barn. (This location would probably have been in the Ritchey backyard about seventy-five to one hundred yards southwest of the house, where even today there is a slight elevation.) Cooper ordered Alexander's Texans, who had remounted and retreated from the ravine below the mill, to take up a position to the right of the battery and behind the stone wall that ran along the road in front of the Ritchey home. Major Bryan's battalion supported the battery on the left, while Hawpe's dismounted cavalry continued to hold the stone barn and the yard immediately in front of the Ritchey house.

Seeing the Confederate artillery drop back, Lynde now brought up his Ninth Kansas Volunteer Cavalry, including Opdyke's howitzers. One company under Captain Henry Flesher was directed to reinforce Mefford on the Federal left, and the balance of the regiment was ordered to support the Ohio artillery, with the mountain howitzers placed alongside Hadley's bigger guns.

Bledsoe's cannoneers came promptly into battery at their new position to contest the Federal advance, "showering grape and canister," according to Colonel Cooper, "among the advancing foe." A fierce duel between Bledsoe's gunners and Hadley and Opdyke's combined artillery raged for half an hour.

Years after the war, a Confederate veteran recalled an incident that happened during the artillery exchange that might have been amusing in the retelling but probably wasn't at the time it happened. A bowlegged captain in Alexander's cavalry regiment, who had placed two or three red Missouri apples in the tail pockets of his coat, was dismounted and standing near Bledsoe's battery when a six-pound solid shot whizzed between his legs, "missing him clean, but shot the tail of his coat off, made pomace of the apples, and ruined his lunch."

The intense artillery duel finally exhausted the Confederate battery's ammunition. In Cooper's words, "Captain Bledsoe, with his artillerymen, stood gallantly to their guns until the last shot was expended."

Dropping back a second time, Bledsoe artillerists limbered about 150 yards to their right rear and, despite having no ammunition, came into battery on a ridge near the road to Camp Coffee. Although the Confederate caissons were empty, the effect of the bluff, according to Cooper, "was at once apparent in checking the Federal cavalry on our left, who had commenced advancing the moment they saw the battery retiring."

With the Federal cavalry moving forward, Jacobi's infantry also advanced up the ravine toward Hawpe's position behind the stone walls surrounding the barn. When the foot soldiers had gotten to within a few hundred yards of the wall, a captain from Colonel Coffee's command, totally unknown to Hawpe but representing himself as an aide to Colonel Cooper, appeared on the scene and started cursing Hawpe's men, calling them cowards, and ordering them to come out from behind the wall and charge. According to Hawpe, the portion of his men who were near "this would-be aide to Colonel Cooper" believed him to be who he said he was and "instantly obeyed the order," leaping over the stone wall to charge the enemy. When a startled Hawpe saw part of his command charging, he assumed they were acting under orders from Colonel Cooper, and he ordered the rest of his men to charge also. (The captain from Coffee's regiment was probably John T. Crisp, who, in fact, did serve as an aide and message bearer for Cooper during the battle.)

The cavalrymen of the Thirty-first Texas "went gallantly into the charge," according to Cooper, and met the infantrymen of the Ninth Wisconsin about one hundred yards beyond the fence in what Cooper called "a sharp fight" and Hawpe termed "a severe conflict." While engaged in the pitched battle with the infantry, the Texans also came under heavy fire from the Federal artillery and were soon forced to retire to their original position behind the stone fence.

Although Hawpe's warriors had momentarily checked the Federal advance, Jacobi's men soon pushed forward again, some of them tramping through the Grabills' lawn. After the war, Mary recalled, "After a sharp encounter, a company of German troops pushed in through the field back of our garden, forced their way through the yard, and making a shield of the hedge in front, fought from there."

The outlook for the Confederates was growing bleak, but Hawpe and his cavalry, lying in wait six or eight deep behind the stone wall, meant to make a last stand. When the Union foot soldiers got to within gunshot range, the

Texans rose up from behind the wall and poured "a perfect stream of fire right into the ranks of the infantry," according to Colonel Lynde.

Back at Camp Coffee, Colonel Shelby had sounded the alarm among the units remaining in camp as soon as he got word that Hawpe's combat team was under attack. He ordered Lieutenant Colonel Tandy Walker of the Choctaw and Chickasaw regiment (Cooper's unit) and Lieutenant Colonel B. Frank Gordon commanding Shelby's Fifth Missouri to march to Newtonia on the double. Walker's Indians led the way as the two regiments galloped toward the battle, their sense of urgency increasing with each boom of the cannons up ahead.

Walker's Choctaws and Chickasaws raced into town "at a full gallop," according to Cooper, just as Hawpe's regiment was making its desperate stand. Cooper directed them to attack the infantry, which was advancing toward the wall to threaten the Texans. Scarcely breaking stride, the Indians passed through the town "singing their war-songs and giving the war-whoop," and Cooper quickly swung into the saddle to help direct the charge. Despite coming under heavy fire from both infantry and artillery, the Indian regiment pressed forward.

Bringing up the rear behind the Choctaws and Chickasaws, Gordon's Missourians, as they approached Newtonia, veered off to challenge Mefford's cavalry on the Confederate right while the Indians poured lead at the Wisconsin foot soldiers. A trooper in Gordon's command who witnessed the Indian charge from afar recollected the scene years after the war:

> *Oh, horrors! That frightful war whoop. The most blood curdling, ear-splitting yell went up that I had ever heard; similar to our modern church solos. Then like an avalanche those furious warriors went at them with demon-like savagery, keeping up that unearthly howl comparable only, in my imagination, to the unhappy shriek of lost souls coming up from the dismal depths of endless torture. Well, that was too much for our friends in blue. The rebel yell would have been like sacred music compared to it.*

Lynde claimed that his infantry met the Confederate assault and returned the fire "nobly," while Cooper said that the two-pronged charge of the Fifth Missouri and the First Choctaw and Chickasaw Regiment "put them to

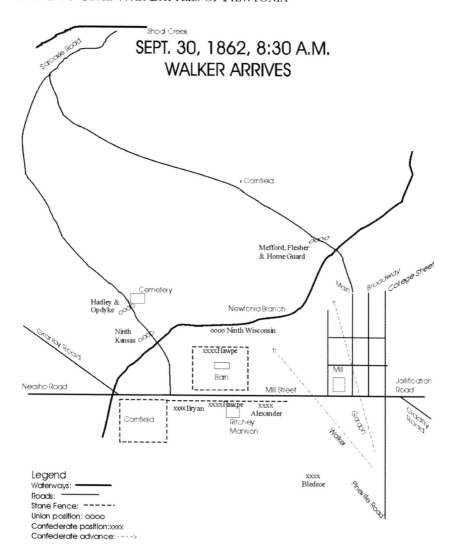

flight." The truth may have been somewhere in between, but at any rate, the Confederate reinforcements soon persuaded the Federals to withdraw, leaving their dead and wounded on the ground.

Realizing that his small force of five hundred men was not going to be able to take Newtonia, Lynde ordered a retreat, and he and his men "slowly retired" toward the Shoal Creek timber about three miles away. They had gone but a short distance down the Sarcoxie road when Lynde was informed that additional Confederate reinforcements had reached Newtonia, and he saw the Southerners "swarming from their concealed positions in the town to harass our retreat." Although the Union withdrawal was orderly at first, Lynde had waited almost too long to sound the retreat. As an anonymous Union observer said, "Almost before our little party were aware of their situation, they were outflanked on either side and almost surrounded. To make good their retreat across a mile and a half of smooth prairie was now a matter of no small difficulty."

Colonel Stevens and his Twenty-second Texas Cavalry, who had heard the cannonading in the early morning and immediately started from Granby toward the sound of the guns, reached the western edge of Newtonia just as the Federals started their retreat. Here Stevens was met by Captain Crisp, who relayed an order from Colonel Cooper to attack the Federal right "in double-quick time," and the Twenty-second Texas promptly carried out the order.

Stevens formed his men in columns of platoons and hurried them forward through a cornfield, breaking down a fence in the process, to try to cut off the Union artillery's retreat. Seeing the Texas cavalrymen about 350 yards on his right flank, Lieutenant Hadley quickly wheeled his battery to the right and, advancing to the top of a hill, "opened fire on them with canister at 250 yards." The Federal guns fired eleven rounds of canister and two solid shot at the Confederates, "scattering their men and horses in every direction," according to Hadley, while Lynde claimed that "the ranks of the enemy were mowed down with great slaughter."

Stevens described the brief encounter more succinctly, saying merely that the Union artillery threw a few rounds in the Texans' direction and then retired "in great haste, leaving their infantry and cavalry to protect their retreat." The Twenty-second Texas eagerly took up the pursuit on the Confederate left, while the Choctaws and Chickasaws pressed forward in the center.

On the right, Colonel Gordon did not immediately press the Confederate advantage because he had momentarily mistaken the Twenty-second Texas for a Union regiment and had begun to form his men to give them battle. This mistake alone may have saved Lynde's combat team from complete annihilation. Cooper sent word to Gordon through two different messengers

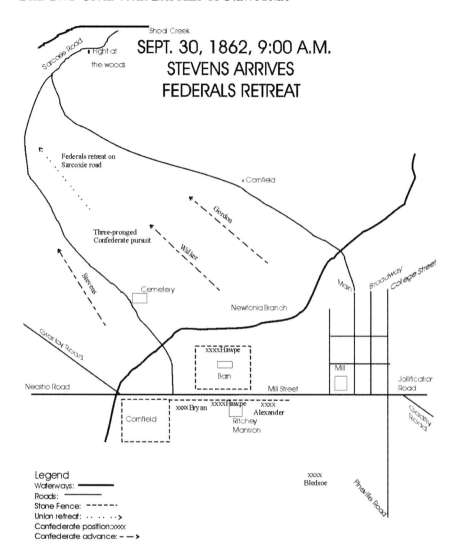

SEPT. 30, 1862, 9:00 A.M.
STEVENS ARRIVES
FEDERALS RETREAT

Shoal Creek

Sarcoxie Road

Fight at the woods

Federals retreat on Sarcoxie road

Cornfield

Gordon

Three-pronged Confederate pursuit

Walker

Stevens

Cemetery

Main

Broadway

College Street

Newtonia Branch

Granby Road

xxxxHawpe

Barn

Mill

Jollification Road

Neosho Road

Mill Street

Godfly Road

Cornfield

xxxxBryan

xxxxHawpe

xxxx Alexander

Ritchey Mansion

Legend
Waterways: ▬▬▬
Roads: ▬▬▬
Stone Fence: ------
Union retreat: ·· ·· ··>
Confederate position:xxxx
Confederate advance: - — >

xxxx Bledsoe

Pineville Road

that the arriving cavalrymen were Southern reinforcements, but by the time the messages were delivered, the delay had "enabled the Federals to get off the field with their batteries and the remnants of their troops." Finally informed of his error, Gordon joined the other two Confederate regiments in the chase after the fleeing Federals.

Hadley's cannons having momentarily checked the Confederate pursuit, Lynde directed the artillery to resume its retreat down the Sarcoxie road, flanked on either side by the cavalry and infantry. The Confederates quickly closed up again to press the pursuit, with the Choctaws in the center, the Missourians on the right, and Stevens's Texans leading the charge on the left. "Now commenced the fight in earnest," reported an anonymous writer to the *Leavenworth Daily Times*. Striving to maintain an orderly withdrawal, Lynde formed and reformed his men several times as they gradually retired. After firing their rifles, the infantry would drop back beyond the cavalry, and the horsemen would hold the line long enough to let the infantry reload before firing their weapons and dropping back just as the infantry had done. The Sixth Kansas Cavalry (Captain Mefford), according to the newspaper correspondent, "kept the enemy at bay" despite being vastly outnumbered and armed only with sabers and revolvers.

When the Federals reached the edge of the timber, the narrowing of the road threw them into a panic as they scrambled to get through the opening in the woods. "About this time," said the *Times* correspondent, "the enemy poured in upon us a murderous fire and drove us back by their overwhelming numbers."

The artillery rumbled through the opening in the woods before the Confederates could surround it, and the Kansas cavalry "drew their sabres and cut their way through" the enclosing circle of the enemy. The infantry, however, was left exposed and scarcely escaped annihilation.

A second correspondent to the *Leavenworth Daily Times* described the retreat in similar terms:

> *Limbering up their guns, the battery moved off. The cavalry and infantry, forming on the right and left, fell back, fighting as they went, the entire distance to the timber, pursued and almost surrounded by apparently countless numbers, who kept up an incessant firing, often at the distance of only a few yards. Fortunately little damage was done until the edge of the timber had been gained; but here some confusion took place owing to the narrowness of the road; and the enemy making a determined rush, the whole party was surrounded. The cavalry and artillery dashed through and escaped, but the infantry were almost entirely cut to pieces or taken.*

In his after-action report, Lynde tried to put the best face on his near-disaster at the edge of the timber. "The enemy…commenced a flank movement on our right and left in overwhelming numbers," he said, and "the fire of the enemy was terrific." His combat team, Lynde claimed, "made a gallant stand, but were overpowered by numbers and obliged to retreat."

After the clash at the edge of the timber, the Confederates chased the Federals another three or four miles and, in Cooper's words, "strewed the woods and road with dead and wounded. Large numbers of arms were also captured, thrown away by the enemy in their flight." All told, according to one Confederate estimate, the pursuit left about fifty Union infantrymen dead (although this may have been an exaggeration). Another eighty Federals were taken prisoner. Most of the captives were soldiers who threw down their arms when they were surrounded at the edge of the timber, while most of the dead were those at the same location who, in Colonel Stevens's words, "refused to surrender" and instead either went down fighting or were shot while dashing for freedom.

Back at the Sarcoxie camp, General Salomon got busy as soon as he heard the early-morning boom of the big guns in the direction of Newtonia. He at once sent a message to Colonel George H. Hall, now in command of Brown's Fourth Brigade Missouri State Militia camped on Center Creek about six miles east of Sarcoxie. (General Brown had been called to Springfield on business.) "Advance immediately toward Newtonia," the dispatch read. "Heavy firing in advance. Send answer by bearer where you will strike the Newtonia road."

Hall had heard the thunder of the artillery himself, but he did not receive Salomon's message until almost 10:00 a.m., by which time the heavy firing had stopped. Aware of General Schofield's admonishment not to risk a defeat and knowing that both General Salomon and Colonel Weer had estimated the size of the Confederate army in the Newtonia area as considerably greater than the combined Federal forces available, Hall was confused as to what the firing had meant in the first place, and now he was doubly confused as to what the lull meant. Not knowing Salomon's intended movements, he nevertheless ordered his brigade to march immediately toward Newtonia by way of Jollification, and he sent a dispatch to Schofield informing the general of his action.

The First Battle of Newtonia: Morning, September 30, 1862

John D. Brown, a soldier in Hall's command, wrote a letter to his sister three days later describing the activity at the Center Creek camp on the morning of September 30:

> *When the battle commenced, we could hear the artillery quite plain. We hitched up immediately and our whole brigade was ready in a short time…*
>
> *Orders soon came to move and away we went, five or six miles on the road.*

When the sounds of the early morning firing at Newtonia did not soon abate, Salomon ordered the Sixth Kansas Volunteer Cavalry under Colonel William R. Judson and the Third Indian Home Guard under Colonel Phillips to "proceed to the battlefield on a trot." Salomon would follow with the infantry and artillery, while about four hundred Indians and two pieces of artillery would stay behind to guard the train.

Judson's Kansans, three hundred strong, turned out on the double and led the march toward Newtonia. About ten miles down the road, just north of Shoal Creek, they came upon Hadley's artillery, Opdyke's mountain howitzers, and some of Lynde's other men "in full retreat before the enemy." The small party, some of whom were bleeding from wounds they'd received in the fight just completed, informed Judson that Colonel Lynde and part of his combat team, including Captain Mefford's company of the Sixth Kansas, were surrounded by the enemy.

Although Phillips and his Indian regiment were lagging behind, Judson decided to press on in hopes of rescuing Lynde and his men. Fearful, however, that the Confederates might have their whole force amassed in the woods south of the stream, he proceeded cautiously. Crossing Shoal Creek, he came to a clearing where a skirmish had obviously taken place. About ten bodies of dead and dying Federal soldiers were strewn on the ground at the edge of a field. They had been completely stripped of their clothing and left to cook in the hot sun, and one report suggested that some of them had also had their throats cut. (This indignity was widely blamed on the Confederate Choctaws.) Judson's men hastily built three or four rail pens and placed the dead soldiers in them to keep the hogs that had already appeared on the scene from mutilating them. While still in the same vicinity, the Kansans captured a Confederate soldier who had strayed from his unit. Resuming the march, Judson soon spotted several other Rebels falling back through the woods toward the prairie. Their "hasty retreat," according to one Union report, was "accelerated very much by the Sharp's rifles of the Sixth."

As soon as he learned of the Union reinforcements, Colonel Cooper opted to withdraw without trying to determine their strength, and he sent out runners to Walker, Gordon, and Stevens with orders to retire. Hurrying ahead to Newtonia to inform the units that had remained there of the new threat and to plot a defense, Cooper was met by fresh troops from Camp Coffee. Colonel Shelby had sent forward Jeans's Missouri Cavalry regiment and Captain Sylvanus Howell's four-gun Eleventh Texas Battery. Howell's battery, supported by Jeans's regiment and Alexander's Thirty-fourth Texas Cavalry, had taken up a position at the graveyard about a half mile north of town. Hawpe's Thirty-first Texas and Bryan's battalion of Cherokees still held the stone wall surrounding and west of Ritchey's barn.

Pursuing the Confederate stragglers through the woods, Colonel Judson did not encounter any resistance until he reached the edge of the prairie. Colonel Stevens's cavalry, bringing up the rear of the Confederate retreat, was drawn up in a line of battle across the Sarcoxie road almost three miles out from Newtonia. Judson at once ordered his cavalry into a line of battle and directed Lieutenant Brainard D. Benedict "to bring his mountain howitzers into position on the gallop." A few shots from Benedict's guns sent the Texans once again racing toward Newtonia, and the Kansans "followed them with a shout to the town." When within "short range" of Newtonia, Benedict again brought his howitzers into battery and commenced shelling the Confederates at the graveyard. Howell's big guns replied with a roar, "using shell and round shot pretty freely." After one of the Federal lieutenants had his horse killed out from under him by a solid shot, Judson quickly decided to "get out of range" because his howitzers were "too light to reply successfully." The Kansans dropped back to some elevated ground about a mile north of the Confederate position at the cemetery, and Judson immediately sent a courier back to General Salomon informing him of the Rebels' position and requesting reinforcements. It was approximately ten o'clock.

For the next several hours, only minor skirmishing among pickets occurred. Cooper used the lull to rest his men and horses, and Captain Bledsoe sent

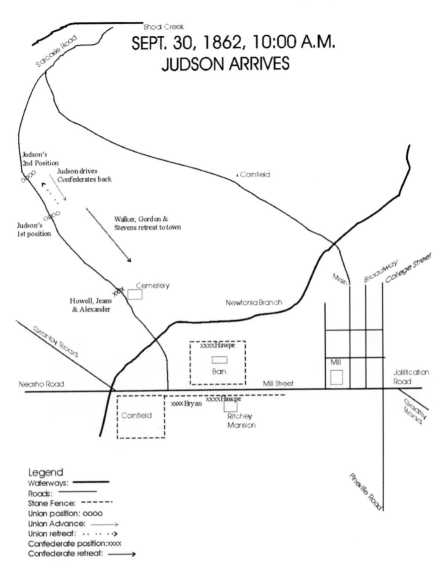

SEPT. 30, 1862, 10:00 A.M.
JUDSON ARRIVES

Shoal Creek

Sarcoxie Road

Judson's
2nd Position

Judson drives
Confederates back

Cornfield

Walker, Gordon &
Stevens retreat to town

Judson's
1st position

Cemetery

Howell, Jeans
& Alexander

Newtonia Branch

Granby Road

Main
Broadway
College Street

Neosho Road

xxxx Hawpe

Barn

Mill

Jollification
Road

Mill Street

Gadfly Road

xxxx Bryan
xxxx Hawpe

Cornfield

Ritchey
Mansion

Pineville Road

Legend
Waterways: ▬▬▬
Roads: ——————
Stone Fence: - - - - - -
Union position: oooo
Union Advance: ———→
Union retreat: ·· ·· ··>
Confederate position: xxxx
Confederate retreat: ┅┅┅→

his caissons back to Camp Coffee for a new supply of ammunition. When Mrs. Ritchey returned home after taking shelter during the morning in the basement of a nearby store, Cooper and some of the other Confederate officers prevailed upon her to fix them something to eat. The exterior of the Ritchey Mansion had been scarred by bullets and cannonballs, and the interior, which had been used during the morning battle by some of the defending Confederates, was in disorder. However, Mrs. Ritchey invited the unwelcome guests in and scrounged up a meal for them. The Ritchey home was also turned into a makeshift hospital, where both Confederate and Federal soldiers were brought for treatment during the battle.

During the noontime lull, Mary Grabill saw some of the Wisconsin infantrymen being marched as prisoners past her house. She imagined that they were some of the same German troops that had charged through her yard earlier in the day.

Realizing that Howell's position at the graveyard north of town was too exposed, Cooper ordered the artillerists and the supporting cavalry back to town. Howell's battery took up a position around Ritchey's stone barn, supported on the right by Alexander's Texans and on the left by Jeans's Missourians. Farther to the left, Bledsoe's battery occupied a position behind the stone wall that ran west of the Ritchey place. After returning from their chase after the Federals, Walker's Indian regiment took up a position on the Rebel right near the mill, and Stevens's Texans extended the left along the stone wall west of the Ritchey home. Gordon's regiment was also placed to the left in support of Bledsoe's artillery. The Confederates then settled in and, in the words of Major Bryan, "quietly and patiently awaited the second attack of the Federal forces."

Chapter 7

The First Battle of Newtonia

Afternoon, September 30, 1862

Shortly after 10:00 a.m., the messenger whom Salomon had sent to Colonel Hall in the early morning caught up with the general along the road to Newtonia bearing a return message from Hall. Although the content of Hall's message is not known, the colonel presumably wanted clarification of Solomon's order to advance toward Newtonia. In response, Salomon dispatched Captain David E. Welch of the Second Ohio Cavalry with a second message to Hall and with instructions for Welch to keep communication open between the two commands.

Continuing the march toward Newtonia, Salomon soon met Federal soldiers retreating from the morning fight who informed him that Lynde had been defeated in his attempt to take the town and the Wisconsin infantry had been "cut up." Salomon hurried forward.

Meanwhile, Colonel Hall continued marching toward Newtonia by way of Jollification. By early afternoon, he had covered about eight miles and still had heard no resumption of the early morning firing in the direction of Newtonia. He had received no further word from Salomon, Captain Welch not having reached him, and therefore he had no knowledge of the general's movements. Suggesting the confusion in the command, John Brown's letter to his sister said, "There was orders from the front not to be in a hurry, then soon again to push forward."

More perplexed than ever, Colonel Hall temporarily halted the southward march. He had no way of knowing the result of the morning engagement but had reason to believe that the Confederates had held Newtonia. He worried that, if he continued toward the town by his present route, the Rebels would be between him and Salomon's troops. After a consultation with his principal officers, Hall determined to head west until he struck the Sarcoxie–Newtonia road, and the march resumed by back roads.

About 2:00 p.m. Colonel Phillips's regiment finally arrived to reinforce the Sixth Kansas Cavalry, "much to our gratification," according to Judson, who had held his position on the high ground north of Newtonia for four hours. Phillips dismounted his command and positioned the Indians in a line of battle alongside the Kansans.

Judson and Phillips held the ridge another hour before Salomon arrived on the field to take charge of the Federal forces. After hearing reports from the two colonels and studying the Confederate position through field glasses, he quickly deployed his forces. He ordered Judson's Sixth Kansas, supported by Benedict's mountain howitzers, to the right along the same ridge the Federals already occupied, and he sent Phillips's Third Indian Home Guards left to the wooded ravine running toward the town, the same ravine the Wisconsin infantry had occupied earlier in the day. Captain Norman Allen's battery and three pieces of Captain Stockton's battery were placed in the center, supported by the First Battalion of the Tenth Kansas Infantry and what remained of the Ninth Wisconsin. The other three pieces of Stockton's battery under Lieutenant Hadley, which had already done service in the morning, were kept behind the line as a reserve, along with the Second Battalion of the Tenth Kansas.

Outnumbered, Solomon was in no hurry to bring on a general engagement until reinforcements arrived. He had received reports from captured prisoners placing the Confederate strength at seven thousand men, while his own force numbered less than half that figure. His plan was merely to keep the Rebels in check with his artillery while he "waited anxiously for the arrival of Colonel Hall." When the Missouri militia reached the field, he would then "advance upon the enemy with the whole force."

As soon as the batteries got into position, the Union cannoneers commenced showering the town with a heavy volley, and the Confederate

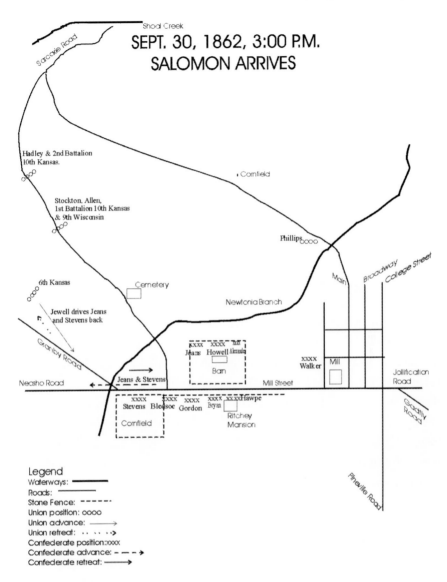

guns near the barn were quick to reply. One Kansas soldier waxed almost poetic in his description of the artillery duel:

> *The artillery—Allen's, Stockton's, and a section (I believe) of Blair's batteries, with six howitzers—took positions and opened fire on the town, which was immediately answered by the rebel battery of six guns only. It*

was a beautiful sight, with just enough excitement to give it a "delicious flavor." It is a beautiful sight, worth risking to see, to witness a fight between artillery, when the whole thing is spread before you in all its terrible realities. The thundering of our own guns, the spiteful reply of the enemy, the peculiarly whizzing music of the shells and shot, as they fly through the air, and the crash of the destructive missiles as they plow up the ground, or, perchance, crash through some animal, gives an excitement better felt than expressed. It is true that when you hear the shells whizzing through the air you cannot tell where they will fall—whether on your own head or some other luckless spectator—but still the sight is worth seeing.

Shortly after the furious exchange of shot and shell began, Captain Stockton saw that one of the Confederate cannons was concealed in Ritchey's stone barn. Having pushed one of their pieces up a dirt ramp and into the second floor of the building, Howell's artillerists were running the gun up to a window to fire and then pulling it back to the interior of the makeshift blockhouse to reload. Hoping to eliminate the menace, Stockton ordered Lieutenant Edward B. Hubbard, in charge of the battery's section of three-inch rifled guns, to fire a few shells into the building. Two of Hubbard's percussion shells scored a direct hit, sailing through the windows and bursting inside the barn. The explosions killed several Confederate artillerists, sent others "jumping out of the windows in every direction," and, according to Stockton, silenced the Rebel cannon for the rest of the day.

A number of Howell's horses were also killed by Federal artillery. Years after the war, a veteran who had been a member of Howell's unit recalled an incident in which two horses were killed by the same round. Private Bill Franklin, wheel driver on the third piece of the battery, was sitting astride his horse during the artillery duel when a percussion shell from a 2.9-inch Parrott rifle struck the horse in the shoulder, barely missing Franklin's leg. The shell penetrated into the horse, "exploding inside the animal, tearing out his entrails and coming out at the flank," mangling the second horse of the two-horse team so badly that it, too, had to be killed as soon as the fighting died down. "The saddle on which Franklin was riding was split into a dozen pieces," remembered the veteran, "and both of his legs were frightfully bruised, but, strange to say, he was not killed."

As the battle raged throughout the day, some of the women and children of the community huddled "for company and safety" at the Grabill home. At first, Mary tried to find places of refuge, like the big fireplaces or the cellar, for her and the others or to move toward the center of the room, but she ended up "standing in the doorway in the familiarity which bred a contempt of danger, in a desire to see what I could." One of the incidents she witnessed, which she still vividly recalled years after the war, was the sight of Martha Ritchey, twenty-year-old daughter of Mathew Ritchey, frantically "wandering about, bare-headed, searching for her father, among a rain of bullets and the noise of the cannon."

After the dueling artillerists had boomed away at each other for some time, Colonel Cooper directed Colonel Stevens and Colonel Jeans to attack the Union right flank. Emerging from the lane formed by the stone fences west of town, the two cavalry regiments formed a battle line and, with Jeans taking the lead, rode out across the prairie along the Neosho road "to feel the position of the enemy," according to Stevens, "ascertain his strength, and draw him out."

Seeing the flanking movement of the Confederate cavalry, Judson's Sixth Kansas, under the immediate command of Lieutenant Colonel Lewis R. Jewell, rode down off the ridge northwest of town to meet the threat. When they came to within about three hundred yards of Jeans's regiment, the Kansans opened fire with their Sharp's carbines, and the Missourians promptly replied. One hundred yards farther to the rear, Stevens held his fire. About the same time, he noticed a second column of Federals, supported by a battery of artillery, approaching on his right in an apparent attempt to cut him off from the town.

The Union cannoneers were Stockton's men, and according to their captain, they got the Rebel cavalry "under an enfilading fire, scattering horses and riders in every direction." Stevens and Jeans quickly ordered a retreat in the face of the artillery.

The Kansans, seeing the withdrawal, drew their sabers and charged down the Granby road after the fleeing Rebels, raising plumes of dust as they galloped across the prairie. Despite the flying pursuit of the Kansans, the Confederate retreat, according to Stevens, was "executed in good order." When the Rebel cavalrymen reached the town, they immediately took cover

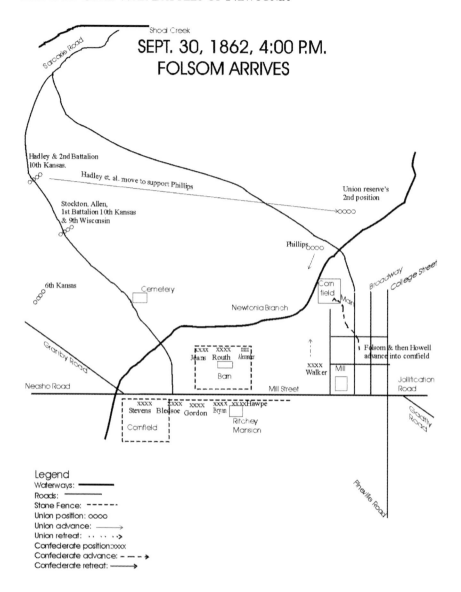

behind the stone wall running west of the Ritchey place and hunkered down in relative safety as missiles from the Federal artillery continued to whizz overhead or burst around them. Jewell's Kansans raced to within about two hundred yards of the entrance to the lane before a few rounds from Bledsoe's battery, supported by Gordon's cavalry, persuaded them to retire to the position on the ridge northwest of town that they had previously held.

Shortly afterward, Confederate lookouts spotted a large body of cavalry coming toward town on their left and rear, and Colonel Cooper sent Stevens to reconnoiter and determine who they were. The new arrivals proved to be Colonel Sampson Folsom and his First Choctaw Regiment, which had left Scott's Mill thirty-five miles away early that morning and reached Newtonia after a hard march.

About the same time, Colonel Phillips's Pin Indians were advancing undetected up the ravine toward the town. Using the brush and plum thickets along Newtonia Branch and the rail fences of a nearby field as cover, they got into position on the Confederate right below the mill and opened a scalding fire on Walker's First Choctaw and Chickasaw Regiment, which was defending that portion of the Rebel line.

Reporting to Cooper just as the fighting near the mill intensified, the newly arrived Choctaws under Colonel Folsom were immediately sent to support Walker's besieged regiment and to try to flank the Federal left. Moving east along Mill Street, Folsom succeeded, by passing through a cornfield undetected, in getting very close to Phillips before the bluecoats even knew of the threat. Folsom's Indians let out a war whoop as they opened fire, and in the words of Colonel Cooper, "the engagement soon became general between the two Choctaw regiments and the jayhawkers and hostile Indians."

As this "most determined fight...in regular Indian style" (as one Union observer described it) raged, the casualties mounted. Captain William Webber and one or two Indian soldiers of the Third Home Guard were killed. In addition, Major John A. Foreman and a number of Federal Indians were wounded. On the Confederate side, Captain Martin Folsom of the First Choctaw Regiment was knocked from his horse gravely wounded and died later in the day.

Noticing that Colonel Phillips's position on the Federal left was being "hotly contested," General Salomon sent up the reserve, the Second Battalion of the Tenth Kansas Infantry and the left half of Stockton's battery under Lieutenant Hadley, to support the Indian regiment. Captain Stockton ordered Lieutenant Hadley to move to a point on Phillips's left, while Stockton directed the fire from the right half of his battery to his left, where the two Choctaw regiments were advancing against the Pins. A few volleys from the big guns soon checked the Confederate advance. As soon as the Rebel line began to waver, the Pin Indians once again pressed forward, pushing the Choctaws and Chickasaws back.

Colonel Cooper recalled the scene in glowing terms in his after-action report two days later:

> *The battle was now raging in all parts of the field. Their masses of infantry could be plainly seen advancing in perfect order, with guns and bayonets glittering in the sun. The booming of cannon, the bursting of shells, the air filled with missiles of every description, the rattling clash of small-arms, the cheering of our men, and the war-whoop of our Indian allies, all combined to render the scene both grand and terrific.*

Seeing the Federal infantry "advancing at double-quick" to reinforce Phillips, Cooper ordered Captain Howell to send two of his artillery pieces to take a position in the cornfield occupied by Colonel Folsom's Choctaws and open on the foot soldiers before they could reach the scene of the fight. Hurrying to the designated spot, Howell's gunners unlimbered and fired a few rounds that scattered the Kansans. At the same time, the remaining guns of Howell's battery, under Lieutenant William A. Routh, were turned toward the Union advance under Phillips, and a few shells bursting among "the jayhawkers and Pin Indians" quickly persuaded them to withdraw.

Captain Stockton, who claimed that the Federal Indians began to retire only after their ammunition gave out, covered the retreat with his artillery. Noticing a large body of Confederates (Folsom's regiment) posted in the cornfield directly in front of the position Phillips's Indians had just vacated, the captain turned his fire on their "condensed masses," and according to Stockton, "the slaughter was terrible." When two percussion shells burst among the Choctaws in the cornfield, they "scattered, and rushing upon a fence, crushed it flat to the ground." Stockton reported that other Confederates, amassed along the stream and about the houses nearby (Walker's regiment), also "suffered greatly from both our solid shot and spherical-case."

Lieutenant Colonel Michael W. Buster's Missouri Battalion (also called Buster's Indian Battalion) had marched from Indian Territory into southern Missouri in late September, and the command was camped at Pineville on

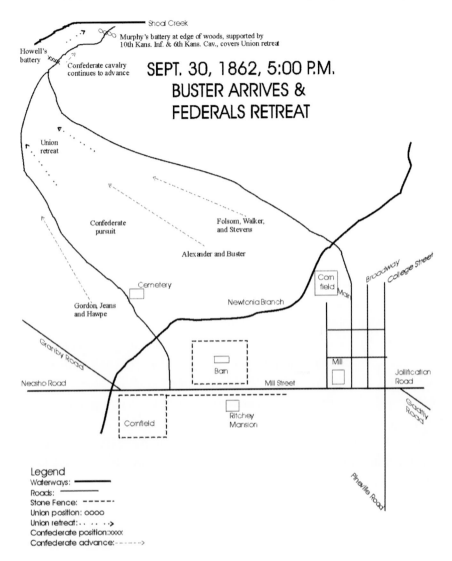

Shoal Creek

Murphy's battery at edge of woods, supported by
10th Kans. Inf. & 6th Kans. Cav., covers Union retreat

Howell's
battery

Confederate cavalry
continues to advance

SEPT. 30, 1862, 5:00 P.M.

BUSTER ARRIVES &

FEDERALS RETREAT

Union
retreat

Confederate
pursuit

Folsom, Walker,
and Stevens

Alexander and Buster

Broadway

College Street

Cemetery

Corn
field

Main

Newtonia Branch

Gordon, Jeans
and Hawpe

Granby Road

Barn

Mill

Jollification
Road

Goodly
Road

Neosho Road

Mill Street

Cornfield

Ritchey
Mansion

Pineville Road

Legend
Waterways: ▬▬▬
Roads: ────
Stone Fence: ------
Union position: oooo
Union retreat: . . .. ..·>
Confederate position: xxxx
Confederate advance: ------->

the morning of September 30 with plans to leave for Camp Coffee at sunrise.
Just as the men were getting ready to start, a private in Captain J. Henry
Minhart's company murdered another member of the same unit, and the
march was delayed while officers investigated the killing. Leaving Minhart's
company behind to bury the dead soldier, Buster's battalion finally started
for Camp Coffee about 11:00 a.m. Six miles north of Pineville, a messenger
rode up and informed Buster of the battle raging at Newtonia.

Stopping his train, Buster issued ammunition to his men and started "at a brisk trot" toward Camp Coffee. About three o'clock in the afternoon, the battalion reached the camp, where Buster allowed his men a brief rest stop to load their weapons. It was an unseasonably hot day, and most of the men also took the opportunity to drink from the spring. After a five-minute break, the march to Newtonia resumed "at a gallop."

Buster reached the field about five o'clock that afternoon, just as Colonel Cooper was redeploying his forces for an all-out assault on the wavering Federals. Cooper assigned Buster to take up a position alongside Alexander's Texans near the center of the Confederate line in support of the artillery. Colonel Stevens's partisans, Walker's Choctaws and Chickasaws, and Folsom's First Choctaw Regiment were thrown out on the right. Colonel Gordon's and Colonel Jeans's Missouri regiments and Hawpe's Thirty-first Texas were placed on the left.

Salomon had planned to advance on Newtonia with his entire force once Hall's Missouri brigade arrived to reinforce him, but when the dilatory militia commander had still not reached the field as darkness approached, the general ordered a retreat. Abandoning their position along the ridge northwest of town, the Federals started back along the Sarcoxie road toward the Shoal Creek timber.

Seeing the Federal withdrawal, Cooper ordered his forces forward and thus began another pursuit across three miles of open prairie. It appeared, in the words of one Union observer, "as if the morning scene were to be re-enacted."

The Federals had been retiring for some time when Salomon, learning of the Confederate pursuit, ordered Captain Stockton to hurry forward to the timber and place his artillery near where the road entered the woods and cover the retreat. Stockton had scarcely gotten into battery when the pursuing Rebels drew up in a line of battle along the ridge that the Federals had lately occupied. "They dressed up their lines, over a mile long," according to Stockton, "but refused to advance or even to come within range of my guns. The sun was now down, but the moon was giving a brilliant light, so that the rebel line was perfectly distinct, when I limbered to the rear and retired into the woods."

It was about 4:00 p.m. when Colonel Hall's brigade finally came out on the Sarcoxie road about eight miles north of Newtonia. Here, Hall met some stragglers from Salomon's command who informed him of the events surrounding the morning battle and told him that Salomon and Weer had marched down to relieve the morning combatants. About the same time, Hall heard a resumption of artillery firing at Newtonia, sounds that told him that Salomon had reached the field and that the battle was once again raging. The militia brigade then started "with all possible dispatch" toward Newtonia. Nearing the battlefield about sunset, Hall met General Solomon's troops "retreating in great confusion."

That there was still some confusion in Hall's command as well is evinced in John Brown's letter to his sister three days later: "We got within a mile or so of the battle field and were ordered to camp, but no sooner in park, than ordered to the field, that the enemy were advancing. Away we dashed to the prairie."

As the last of the retiring Federals disappeared into the Shoal Creek woods, the advancing Confederates once again drew up in an impressive line of battle about a mile long along a ridge about a quarter mile from the timber. Here Howell's guns came promptly into battery and opened fire. A retreating Kansas soldier recalled, "A volley of shells went screaming and tearing through the timber over our heads."

Colonel Weer at once ordered the Sixth Kansas Cavalry and the Tenth Kansas Infantry to countermarch, and according to the same Kansas soldier, "notwithstanding the men had been marching and fighting without food or water since early morning, they obeyed the order with alacrity and formed promptly in front of the enemy."

Having reached the field at about this time, Colonel Hall received instructions from Salomon to cover his retreat, and the Missouri brigade "also dashed forward with a shout to the prairie." The militia commander ordered his unit to draw up in a battle line just beyond the timber, and he placed Captain David Murphy's Battery F of the First Missouri Light Artillery, under command of Lieutenant James Marr, in a position at the edge of the woods so that the location of the big guns was masked by the thick foliage of the blackjack and post oak sprouts clumped together at the edge of the prairie. To the Confederates, the woods were now a picture of darkness, but the Federals arrayed at the edge of the timber could still make out the Confederate cavalry approaching across the prairie. When the grayclads were only a couple hundred yards away, Marr's artillery opened fire but, according to Colonel Cooper, "owing to the darkness did little execution."

The flash of the guns, however, gave the Confederates the location of the Federal artillery, and Captain Howell "threw a few shells into them, fired somewhat at random, but which it was afterwards ascertained exploded among them." Although the exploding shells injured only one man, they caused a minor panic among Weer's battle-weary Kansas troops, and the Federals, according to Cooper, "now fled in confusion, leaving the road, passing through fields and woods, and abandoning loaded wagons by the way wedged between trees."

Not wishing to press the pursuit in the darkness, Cooper ordered his forces back to Newtonia, while the Federals continued to draw off toward Sarcoxie. The Confederates had gotten about halfway back to town when an express rider galloped up to Colonel Buster, whose command formed the rear guard, and reported that Walker's Choctaw and Chickasaw unit was still in the woods and unaware of the Confederate retreat. Buster immediately sent the rider back to order the wandering Indians in. Meanwhile, many of the exhausted Federals camped north of Shoal Creek on the night of the thirtieth. A rainstorm moved in during the wee hours of the next morning, breaking the heat of the previous day and drenching the bivouacking soldiers, who then resumed the march to Sarcoxie.

The First Battle of Newtonia had, in Colonel Cooper's words, "lasted from sunup until dark, with the exception of an interval of two hours," and it ended as a Confederate victory. The Federals were repulsed in both of their attempts to storm the town, and they were driven three miles back across the prairie in each case. Comparing the number of casualties on each side, however, is an inexact science, since General Salomon did not quantify his loss, but it is safe to say that the Federals suffered considerably greater casualties than the Confederates. Colonel Cooper reported his losses at 2 officers and 10 enlisted men killed, 13 officers and 50 enlisted men wounded, and 3 enlisted men missing, for a total of 78 casualties. General Salomon, meanwhile, said only that Colonel Lynde's troops in the morning engagement were "defeated and the infantry cut up," while in the afternoon fight the Federal loss "was very small." Colonel Weer gave perhaps the best indication of the Federal loss when he said in his after-action report,

First Battle of Newtonia marker on the grounds of the Ritchey Mansion.

"Four whole companies of the Ninth Wisconsin, except about ten men, are killed, wounded, or captured, besides others of the Sixth and Ninth Kansas and Third Indian." Most historians have estimated the number of Federal casualties in the neighborhood of 250, while the actual Confederate loss may have been as high as 100.

It is also difficult to determine with any precision the number of Federal and Confederate combatants engaged in the battle, since both sides tended to overestimate the enemy's numbers while downplaying their own. However, General Schofield placed the total number of Federals involved in the Newtonia action, including Hall's meandering brigade, at 4,500 men, and this seems a credible estimate. Cooper, on the other hand, claimed his own force "did not exceed 4,000 men during any part of the day," but this figure seems somewhat low. Federal estimates of Confederate strength ranged from 5,000 to 11,000, with most estimates in the 7,000 to 8,000 range. The actual figure was probably between 4,000 and 7,000 but nearer to 4,000 than 7,000.

General Salomon and Colonel Hall devoted a large part of their after-action reports to blaming each other for the Federals' lack of success at

Newtonia. "Why Colonel Hall did not come in time," complained Salomon, "and on the road he reported he would come, is a mystery to me, and can be explained perhaps only by him. There is no doubt but that we could have annihilated the enemy if he had appeared in time and on the proper road." Hall, on the other hand, said that the early morning message from Salomon was the only communication he received from the general, and he attributed his tardiness to the vague instructions the message contained. He also suggested that only his fortuitous arrival just as the Kansas brigades were in full retreat saved Salomon's rear from utter annihilation. "I was entirely without information of the intention of General Salomon," Hall groused. "I desired him to send me a messenger. He neither sent me a messenger or a line, nor did he communicate with me in any way until I reached the battlefield." Salomon's rear, Hall told General Brown, "must have been captured and destroyed but for the timely arrival of your brigade."

Whereas the Federal leaders wasted a good deal of writing paper griping about each other, Colonel Cooper devoted several hundred words of his report to praising the conduct of his men. "The thanks of the country are due the troops engaged in this battle," he concluded, "for the bravery and coolness displayed in the face of an enemy greatly their superior in numbers."

Chapter 8

The Federals Retake Newtonia

All of the troops of Salomon's and Weer's brigades made it back to Sarcoxie by the morning of October 1, and Colonel Hall also reported to Salomon at Sarcoxie on the same morning. When he learned that Salomon did not intend to renew the attack, Hall marched his troops to their camp on Center Creek six miles east of Sarcoxie.

On the evening of September 30, General Blunt had forwarded most of the troops of his division that were still at Fort Scott to Sarcoxie to reinforce Salomon and Weer. After dispatching messages to General Curtis and General Schofield pledging the cooperation of his division with the Missouri troops and promising to personally meet Schofield in the field, Blunt himself started for Sarcoxie with a small escort on the morning of October 1. Arriving the next day, he took command of his division.

Upon learning early on the morning of October 1 of Salomon's failed attack at Newtonia, General Totten, who was camped outside Springfield with his First Division, Army of Southwest Missouri, started west at once to support the Federal troops near Sarcoxie. Later the same morning, General Schofield left Springfield, overtook Totten along the road, and proceeded with Totten's command to Hall's camp on Center Creek, arriving on the evening of October 2.

The next morning, Blunt met Schofield at the Center Creek camp, now dubbed Camp Curtis, and Schofield issued orders directing the movements of the Federal troops against the Confederates at Newtonia. General Blunt's Kansas division and General Totten's Missouri division, each about six thousand strong, were ordered to march from their respective camps at eight o'clock on the evening of October 3 via separate roads and, operating in conjunction with each other, to launch a coordinated attack against the Confederates at Newtonia at dawn of the next day. If either force, for whatever reason, was unable to carry out the attack at the designated time, the commanding general of that force would immediately send a runner notifying the commanding general of the other force.

Blunt divided his troops into two columns for the march to Newtonia. Taking the Sarcoxie–Newtonia road, Blunt and the main column would approach Newtonia from the north, following the same route his soldiers had used on September 30. Meanwhile, a strong detachment would march toward Granby with plans to approach Newtonia from the west.

General Schofield would accompany Totten's command, which would march from its Center Creek camp via Jollification and approach Newtonia from the east. Schofield planned to trap the Confederates in a three-pronged pincer movement.

Following the Federal defeat on September 30, Colonel Cooper decided to change his headquarters from Camp Coffee to the Shoal Creek area north of Newtonia or near Granby, and he ordered Colonel Shelby to move forward with his brigade on the Sarcoxie road, find a location that would prove suitable for the entire command, and camp there until the rest of the division could come up. Cooper learned almost immediately that the Federals were receiving heavy reinforcements from Springfield. He urgently appealed to General Rains for reinforcements of his own, but when none were forthcoming, Shelby was ordered back to Newtonia.

On the late afternoon of October 3, Confederate scouts reported the advance of a Federal force on the Jollification road. About the same time, a dispatch from General Rains reached Colonel Cooper ordering him to fall back, and he immediately began making preparations to retreat. Hoping to buy time for the withdrawal of his main force, Cooper sent Shelby to attack the Federal advance on the Jollification road, and he ordered Lieutenant Colonel Buster to march with his battalion and Major Bryan's Cherokee battalion to Granby and resist any Federal movement from Sarcoxie via that route.

A detachment of Shelby's command rode out on the Jollification road all the way to Jollification, where it attacked and captured some Federal pickets, but the rapid advance of Totten's division forced it to retreat immediately. Leaving the prisoners at a blacksmith shop, Shelby's men returned promptly to Newtonia.

Meanwhile, Buster reached Granby with his detachment of about four hundred men about 6:30 p.m. on October 3. After posting pickets along three roads north of town near Shoal Creek, Buster fell back to Granby with the main force and settled in for what promised to be "a good night's rest." Between 1:00 and 2:00 a.m., however, a rider arrived from Camp Coffee carrying a dispatch from Colonel Cooper requesting information about whether there had been any movement of the enemy in the direction of Granby. Buster sent out scouts on the main Sarcoxie road to try to obtain the requested information, and when they got to within about three hundred yards of where Major Bryan was camped with a detachment of pickets, the scouts heard considerable firing. Assuming the firing to be an exchange between Bryan's men and the Federal advance, the scouts hurried back to Granby and reported to Buster, who immediately roused his men and ordered them to their horses. They had just finished mounting when a courier from Major Bryan galloped in confirming that a large but undetermined force of the enemy, supported by artillery, was approaching Granby and that the pickets had skirmished with the Federal advance. Major Bryan and the pickets rode in moments later, having fallen back on the town as previously instructed to do if they encountered the enemy in force.

With his entire command now collected at Granby, Buster rode back out on the main Sarcoxie road about a quarter of a mile and again skirmished with the advancing Federals. The "firing became general and rapid on both sides," but when one of Buster's captains had his horse killed from under him and a ball shot through his hat, the colonel decided it was time to retire. Falling back through Granby and forming at "an advantageous place" on the Newtonia road about a half mile out of town, Buster and his men watched with steely nerves as the large force of Federals marched out of Granby, flanked them without offering battle, and continued toward Newtonia just as light began to streak the eastern sky and rain started pouring down. Marching south over a ridge "by a double-quick movement," Buster disappeared from Federal view, soon struck the Neosho–Newtonia road, and arrived back at Newtonia ahead of the Federals he had encountered at Granby.

The Confederate skirmishers had caused minimal delay in the Federal march, but they had confirmed what Colonel Cooper already suspected. A Union force greatly superior to his own was advancing toward Newtonia. Early on the morning of October 4, he ordered Shelby to send his supply train back to Camp Coffee so that the retreat could commence. To delay the Federal pursuit, Shelby would continue to hold Newtonia as long as feasible and then cover the retreat as a rear guard.

Finding that "no officer appeared to be in command" when he reached Newtonia, Lieutenant Colonel Buster promptly ordered Captain Howell's artillery into position to meet the approaching Federals, and he deployed his own battalion to support the battery on the left. As the defense was still being organized, Colonel Shelby appeared and took command, and he sent Jeans's regiment to support the battery's right. The Confederates maintained this defensive position for about fifteen minutes before Shelby received a report that communication with Camp Coffee was cut off by Federals who were threatening the Pineville road to his rear, and he promptly ordered a retreat. Using a secondary road west of the main Pineville road, the Confederates started south, with Shelby commanding the right wing and Buster the left.

Unlike four days earlier, when the Federal attack had taken the citizens of Newtonia by surprise, Mary Grabill and the other women of the community were warned early on the morning of October 4 of the impending Federal assault. Mary and some of her acquaintances gathered a few personal items and set out across the prairie with their children to find a place that was out of danger. Years after the war, Mary recalled what happened next:

> About a mile out of town, we saw approaching on the open prairie an immense body of cavalry—thirty thousand in number altogether. They came at double-quick, and we were so terrified we did not know what to do—especially as in their rear their artillery was shelling the Southerners, who were retreating toward the south as rapidly as possible, and these shells

Mary Grabill, circa 1890.
Courtesy of Larry James.

*went woo-o-shing over our heads just as though aimed at us. And we were
by no means sure in our own minds that they were not. We fell down in
the cover of a zigzag fence, and taking white things out of our bags, waved
them as flags of truce!*

As Mrs. Grabill rightly recalled, the Confederates were already in retreat
when, in the words of Colonel Cooper, "the main body of the Federal Army
made its appearance before Newtonia shortly after sunrise and commenced
a furious bombardment of the little village." Upon the predetermined firing
of a signal gun, all the batteries of the combined Federal forces, consisting
of thirty-six field guns and four twelve-pound howitzers, opened an intense
artillery fire on the town from three sides.

About the time the artillery bombardment began, Colonel Cooper, like
Colonel Shelby, received a report that communication between Camp
Coffee and Newtonia had been cut off. Leaving Colonel Sampson Folsom

and his Choctaw regiment at Camp Coffee to cover the retreat of the train from that point, Cooper marched toward Newtonia with his own Choctaw and Chickasaw regiment and Stevens's Texans to reopen communication. Approaching the town, he found that, although communication had not been completely cut off as reported, Colonel Shelby had already withdrawn.

Only a few skirmishers of the Federal advance occupied the Pineville road between Newtonia and the Indian Creek timber, but to their rear something more menacing drew Colonel Cooper's attention. After pounding Newtonia with artillery for about thirty minutes, General Schofield had ordered a charge, and Cooper could now "plainly see large masses of infantry descending the high ridge north of the town."

Filing to the west, Cooper took the same secondary road by which Colonel Shelby had retired and began retreating south toward the Indian Creek timber. Schofield promptly pushed forward his cavalry and light howitzers to harass the Confederate retreat. As the Confederates neared the timber, Cooper sent Lieutenant Colonel Simpson N. Folsom with a portion of the First Choctaw and Chickasaw Regiment to attack the Federal advance, driving them back and, according to Cooper, killing several. The Rebels then withdrew into the timber and took up positions of ambush along the Pineville road, which followed Indian Creek in a southwesterly direction below Camp Coffee. In response, the Federals drew up in a battle line on the prairie between Newtonia and the timber and began shelling the woods from a distance but doing little damage.

Cooper sent Captain Sampson Loering's company of the Choctaw and Chickasaw regiment back to Camp Coffee to bring off the stragglers and to see what had become of Colonel Sampson Folsom's command. Loering soon returned with the "lagging wagons, stragglers, and women, but could give no account of Colonel Sampson Folsom and his command, who, it seems, had quit his post" and was already in retreat ahead of the main Confederate force. Cooper maintained his position at the edge of Oliver's Prairie until the last of the stragglers from Camp Coffee had passed, and then he and the rest of his command resumed their retreat along the Indian Creek road until it intersected the Neosho to Pineville road. Here the Confederates turned south and camped on the night of October 4 at Dog Hollow, four miles north of Pineville.

Over the next several days, the Federal advance followed the retreating Confederates, driving them into Arkansas, while the main Union force remained near Newtonia. General Schofield had originally planned merely to push the Confederates out of Newtonia and then occupy southwest Missouri until reinforcements from Rolla and Fort Leavenworth could reach him. Information gained at Newtonia, however, convinced him that, even though his troops might be outnumbered, they were better equipped and better prepared than Hindman's army in northwest Arkansas, and he decided to move against the Confederates without further delay. Marching toward Cassville, he ordered General Francis J. Herron to meet him there with all the available forces left at Springfield. Schofield reached Cassville on October 12, and Herron arrived on the fourteenth. The combined command, now designated the Army of the Frontier, then started toward Arkansas on the Wire Road and reached Pea Ridge on October 17.

Meanwhile, Cooper had effected a junction with General Rains at Mud Town (near present-day Lowell, Arkansas). Rains ordered Colonel Shelby's brigade to take up a position at nearby Cross Hollows, and he also detached the Texas regiments from Cooper's command. He sent Cooper's diminished force, which still included Howell's battery, to Indian Territory via Maysville with orders to consolidate the Indian regiments, march to Kansas, and attack Fort Scott. Rains himself retreated with the infantry toward Huntsville.

Upon arrival at Pea Ridge, General Schofield sent out a reconnaissance party, which returned on October 18 carrying news of the Confederate division of forces, and he immediately sent General Blunt with Colonel Weer's and Colonel Cloud's brigades in pursuit of Cooper. Meanwhile, Schofield accompanied General Totten's and General Herron's divisions in pursuit of Rains, and General Salomon's brigade remained at Pea Ridge.

Cooper arrived on the seventeenth at Old Fort Wayne, near Maysville, but he encountered difficulty consolidating his forces. The wayward Colonel Sampson Folsom, who had previously been ordered to meet Colonel Stand Watie at Old Fort Wayne, was thirty miles to the south, and some of Watie's men were also away on an expedition. Colonel D.N. McIntosh's Creek regiment and Lieutenant Colonel Chitty McIntosh's Creek battalion were camped in the area, but only the latter reported promptly. Before Cooper could gather his forces, Blunt attacked him at Old Fort Wayne on the morning of October 22, soundly defeating him and capturing all the guns of Howell's battery.

Meanwhile, Totten and Herron pursued Rains almost all the way to Huntsville before calling off the chase when they became convinced that the Confederates were not going to give them battle.

Later in the year, on December 7, Herron and Blunt met Hindman at the Battle of Prairie Grove. Although the two sides fought each other to a virtual draw, the Confederates, running low on ammunition and food, withdrew from the field when night came on, handing the Federals a strategic victory that gave them an inroad into Arkansas and solidified their hold on Missouri. Although the First Battle of Newtonia had been a short-lived Confederate victory, the South was ultimately unsuccessful in its attempt to establish an enduring presence in Missouri. By the end of 1862, the little town of Newtonia, like the state as a whole, was once again in the firm control of the Union.

Chapter 9

A Nice Clean Little Town

Newtonia, Fall 1862 to Fall 1864

After the Federals drove the Confederates out of Newtonia on October 4, Mary Grabill and her friends wandered back across the prairie to town "picking up quantities of 'shin-plasters' which strewed the ground the Confederates had gone over." The shinplasters Mary spoke of were small-denomination bills issued by the Federal government, and the Rebel soldiers had discarded them during their flight because they knew the fractional currency would be worthless in the South.

Back home, Mary found that nothing but food had been disturbed or taken from her house, because "the hurry had been too great to warrant pillage or other destructing mischief." During the next days and weeks, with Federal authority firmly reestablished, Mary and the other citizens of Newtonia "began to feel more settled in our minds and modes of living."

Thomas Murray, an Iowa soldier camped at Newtonia only a few days after the Rebels had been driven out, seemed to reflect the newfound calm when he told his parents in a letter back home that he was "just laying hear wating for marching orders. This is the best land I have seen in Missiouri," he added. "Newtonia is a nice clean little town but it dont take many houses hear to make a town."

Federal authorities had recognized the strategic location of Newtonia and had established temporary camps there from time to time throughout 1862, but the September 30 battle increased the importance in their minds of establishing a permanent post at the town. General Schofield and General Curtis began discussing the idea in October while Schofield's troops were still busy pursuing the Confederates into Arkansas. Curtis told Schofield in a late October message that if General Blunt stayed in Arkansas much longer, "it will be necessary to have an outpost somewhere near Newtonia."

The following month, Colonel John F. Phillips, with eight companies of the Seventh Missouri State Militia Cavalry, was stationed at Newtonia. In late November, the post was threatened by several hundred of Quantrill's irregulars, who had gone south for the winter earlier in the month and temporarily attached themselves to Shelby's command in northern Arkansas. Roaming back into Missouri, they came to within a few miles of Newtonia but declined to launch an attack when they learned that additional Federal troops, responding to Phillips's request for reinforcements, were on their way to the post.

Colonel Phillips and his regiment were reassigned to Elkhorn Tavern (i.e. Pea Ridge) on December 9, but a succession of other commands took their place so that Newtonia became a semipermanent Federal post. As Mary Grabill remembered, "After the retreat of Cooper's men, we were for a long time under Federal authority."

First in the line of successors to Colonel Phillips was Major Edward B. Eno, whose Eighth Missouri State Militia Cavalry arrived later in December and began work on a blockhouse and stockade. The area around Newtonia and Neosho had been noted by General Curtis two months earlier as a notorious "rebel haunt," and Eno spent much of his time trying to root out the guerrillas. One of Eno's foes of particular note was Jasper County guerrilla Tom Livingston, with whom the major had several skirmishes during the early months of 1863. When they weren't out on scouts after guerrillas, Eno's men continued their work at the Newtonia post, which, by March 1863, consisted of "dirt and stone fortifications, covering about four or five acres."

According to legend, young Myra Maybelle Shirley (later Belle Starr) paid a visit to Newtonia in early 1863 while Major Eno was using the Ritchey home as his headquarters. Several variations of the legend exist, but the common thread of all of them is that the pretty, teenaged Myra Belle, sent to

"Black Room" of the Ritchey Mansion, where Myra Maybelle Shirley was held.

town as a Confederate spy, came riding in on horseback and, while visiting the Ritchey home, entertained the family and their guests by playing the piano. A popular version of the legend says that, after Myra Belle learned that the Federals at Newtonia were planning to attack a party of Confederates at Carthage that included her brother, Major Eno discovered the young girl's mission and confined her in the second-floor "Black Room" of the Ritchey home, so called because the floor had been painted black to cover up the bloodstains that were left from its service as a hospital room during the First Battle of Newtonia. Assuming that the planned attack would be carried out before Miss Shirley could possibly reach Carthage, Eno released her the next morning, but Myra Belle, donning a blue riding skirt and cutting a few switches from a nearby clump of cherry bushes, quickly mounted her horse. Remarking that she would beat the "Feds" to Carthage, she gave her horse a sharp lash with one of the switches, galloped away, and reached her brother and his compatriots in time to warn them of the impending attack.

On April 23, Major Eno was joined at Newtonia by Lieutenant Colonel Thomas T. Crittenden of the Seventh Missouri State Militia Cavalry, as the

Federals continued to fortify the town. Crittenden took command of the post by virtue of his higher rank. At least one soldier in Eno's command had mixed feelings about the arrival of the reinforcements. "I do not know at this time how long we will stay at this post," Thomas J. Divine told his brother in a letter on April 24. "The 7th M.S.M., one battalion of it, come to this place yesterday but I don't know whether they did come to relieve us of this place or not, though I hope not, for I had ruther stay here than any place I ever have been stationed at since I have been in the service."

At the end of April, Colonel Crittenden reported over seven hundred soldiers assigned to the Newtonia post with almost five hundred present on the day of the report. The post's defenses included two pieces of field artillery.

Colonel Crittenden, who became governor of Missouri after the war, boarded at the Ritchey house when he first came to Newtonia. Later, he and his family made their home at the Grabill house, and years afterward Mary recalled the experience as one of her few pleasant memories of the war.

Thomas Divine's blissful days at Newtonia, on the other hand, were numbered. Toward the end of May, Major Eno and his command left Newtonia for a new assignment at Greenfield, and Eno was replaced by Captain Milton Burch of the Eighth Missouri State Militia Cavalry. About the same time, Colonel John F. Phillips returned to Newtonia and reassumed command of the post. A correspondent of the *St. Louis Tri-Weekly Republican* arrived on the colonel's heels, and his report of the situation as he found it at Newtonia on June 5 reflected the same sense of pleasantness that both Mary Grabill and Private Divine experienced:

> *On my arrival here, Col. Phillips had just come down from Greenfield with the First Battalion of his regiment to join Lieut. Col. Crittenden, then in command of this post. The latter officer, in conjunction with Major Eno, of the Eighth Cavalry, M.S.M., have been doing the work up for the rebels, just as it should have been done. This being an extreme outpost of our lines, the rebels make very many efforts to annoy and harrass our men, but sometimes find that it is a two-handed game, played with as high a hand on the opposite side. In the recent engagement Livingston had with the troops of this place, "he got a little more than he bargained for." Several of our men were killed and others wounded, while it was known at the time*

that eight of his (Livingston's) hell-hounds had paid their last debt; since, however, it has been ascertained beyond a doubt that no less than fifteen of their number were killed.

The health and spirits of the command here is very good.

Parties are sometimes given in this town, and dancing (where is the soldier not capacitated for this enjoyment?) is a decidedly healthy exercise, as well as an innocent amusement for all classes and ages of the "genus homo." This is a well known fact, and conceded by all parties, even by the soldiers.

There are some wounded men in the hospital here, and occasionally a case of malarial fever. Disease is often (and, indeed, it might be said, always) kept out of camp by strict cleanliness and a careful observance of the rules of cooking in the preparation of the rations.

Newtonia is quite a pleasantly situated town; a most beautiful site for a large village, but minus the improvements. It was planned and arranged by Judge Ritchey, a prominent Union man, (now member of the State Senate from this district), who has suffered much from these troubles...He owns a very desirable farm here; well improved; has a large steam flouring mill, and by his energy, the business houses of this place were built, as was also the large and spacious seminary that would do honor to a place of larger growth. He is truly the architect of Newtonia.

At the end of June, Colonel Phillips reported six companies of the Seventh Missouri State Militia Cavalry under Crittenden and two companies of the Eighth under Burch assigned to the post at Newtonia.

In late July, Phillips departed Newtonia on special assignment to track down Colonel Coffee and his would-be Confederate troops, which for some time had been roaming throughout southwest Missouri in no apparent hurry to join the regular Southern army in Arkansas. Captain Charles B. McAfee (who later married Martha Ritchey) succeeded Phillips at Newtonia, bringing with him a battalion of the Sixth Missouri State Militia Cavalry.

About the first of October 1863, Coffee made a junction near the Arkansas line with Colonel Shelby, who was moving up to invade Missouri. On the morning of the fourth, Captain McAfee was ordered to join Major A.A. King in the field between Neosho and Pineville to meet the Confederate

Major Mathew Ritchey.
Courtesy of Larry James.

threat. At the same time, Major Eno was ordered to march from Cassville, and Captain Henry V. Stall of the Sixth Missouri State Militia Cavalry was ordered to march from Neosho to replace McAfee at Newtonia.

Arriving at Neosho, McAfee took shelter in the courthouse as Shelby approached the town with about 1,500 men. Under the threat of being shelled out by the superior force, McAfee, after much parleying, surrendered his train and his entire detachment of 180 men.

Meanwhile, Federal forces were concentrating at Newtonia to operate against Shelby. Stall arrived on the fourth, and Eno got there about four o'clock the next morning, as did a detachment of the Seventh Provisional Enrolled Missouri Militia under Colonel John D. Allen. Later on the fifth, Major King marched in, and some of McAfee's men, captured at Neosho but since paroled, also arrived, making a total force of about 550 Federal soldiers at Newtonia.

Shelby was driven out of Missouri in late October, and most of the troops that had gathered at Newtonia to operate against him turned their attention to other pursuits. Mathew Ritchey's son, James M. Ritchey, who had previously organized a company for the Union army and been given the rank of captain, was stationed at Newtonia, in command of Company K of the Seventh Provisional Enrolled Missouri Militia. Captain Ritchey, like several of his predecessors at Newtonia, spent most of his time scouring for bushwhackers and occasionally skirmishing with them. His first lieutenant, Robert H. Christian, was especially zealous in his campaign against guerrillas and Confederate sympathizers, and he had already developed a villainous reputation among Southern-leaning citizens by the time Ritchey's unit was stationed at Newtonia.

Captain James M. Ritchey. *Courtesy of Larry James.*

In mid-January 1864, Captain Ritchey was ordered to Keetsville (now Washburn), located about eight miles southwest of Cassville on the Wire Road, to protect telegraph communication between Fayetteville, Arkansas, and Springfield. He and his company returned to Newtonia in mid-February, but they were again called away shortly afterward. Fearful that Newtonia was once again going to be left to the mercy of marauding gangs, Judge Ritchey, who the previous year had served briefly as a paymaster in the Union army with a rank of major, petitioned Major General William S. Rosecrans, General Curtis's successor in command of the Department of the Missouri, for additional Federal protection in southwest Missouri. Rosecrans responded on March 22 that it was not proper for him to discuss the disposition of forces, but soon afterward, the judge's son was returned with his unit to Newtonia.

On May 19, 1864, Captain Ritchey's men skirmished with Quantrill's band of guerrillas, although Ritchey mistook them for regular Confederate soldiers under Brigadier General John S. Marmaduke. Quantrill was on his way north after spending the winter in Texas, and the next day his band attacked a small home guard force at Lamar. The same day, May 20, Ritchey reported his previous-day's set-to with the guerrillas to both Fort Scott and Springfield, and he fretted that the Federal army might again abandon Newtonia. His father and E.H. Grabill dispatched a letter to Federal authorities, also on the twentieth, expressing the same concern. Brigadier General John B. Sanborn, commanding the District of Southwest Missouri, responded to Captain Ritchey three days later, assuring him that Newtonia would not be deserted, and it continued to serve as a Federal post throughout most of the remainder of the war.

Chapter 10

Price's Invasion of Missouri

From the time General Sterling Price was driven out of Missouri in early 1862, he longed to reenter his home state to try to reclaim it for the South. In August 1864, after two and half years, Confederate authorities finally approved such an undertaking, and Price was given command of the expedition.

Previous raids led by other Confederate officers from Missouri had ended in defeat. General Marmaduke's cavalry had been repulsed during two separate forays in the winter and spring of 1863, and Colonel Shelby had been driven from the state in October of the same year. But Price's incursion was to be not merely a cavalry raid but also a full-scale invasion and an all-out effort to retake Missouri for the South. His army consisted of three divisions under Marmaduke, Shelby (who had been promoted to brigadier general), and Major General James F. Fagan, totaling about twelve thousand men and three batteries of artillery. About one-third of the men were unarmed, as Price was forced to fill out his command with conscripts, deserters, and other irregulars; however, if his mission proved successful, thousands of Southern-leaning Missourians would view him as a liberator and flock to his army, bolstering his numbers and also bringing additional weapons.

Organization of Price's army was completed in mid-September at Pocahontas, Arkansas. After crossing the border into southeast Missouri on

General Sterling Price. *Courtesy of J. Dale West.*

September 19, Price marched north toward St. Louis, headquarters of the Union's Department of the Missouri. On the twenty-seventh, Fagan's and Marmaduke's divisions attacked a Federal force of a little over one thousand men who were entrenched at Fort Davidson near Pilot Knob under Brigadier General Thomas Ewing Jr. Despite a vast superiority in numbers, the Confederates were repulsed with heavy casualties. Ewing then added insult to injury when he spiked his heavy artillery guns so that they would be of no use to the enemy, set a slow fuse to his magazine so that his munitions would explode after he was gone, and slipped off undetected in the middle of the night before Price could bring up all of his forces for a second, more determined attack the next day.

Although Ewing was forced to withdraw in the face of overwhelming Confederate numbers, the unexpected resistance and delay that Price encountered at Pilot Knob forced him to reevaluate his plan to march on St. Louis. Instead, he veered northwest toward Jefferson City, occasionally skirmishing with Federal cavalry along the way. By the time he got to the state capital on October 7, Union reinforcements had arrived, and the

Southerners declined to launch an assault. Bypassing Jefferson City, Price marched west along the Missouri River toward Kansas City with a large body of Federal troops under Major General Alfred Pleasonton, composing a provisional cavalry division, in dogged pursuit.

Meanwhile, General Curtis, now commanding the Department of Kansas, prepared to meet the Confederates as they neared Kansas City. His advance under General Blunt started skirmishing with the approaching grayclads on October 19 near Lexington, and over the next few days Blunt and Price fought a series of minor battles, including actions at the Little Blue River and at Independence. Although the Federals were forced in each case to retire in the face of the advancing Rebel army, the actions allowed Pleasonton to close in on Price's rear, threatening to trap the Confederates between two large Union forces.

Price's army had been reduced by desertion, disease, and battlefield casualties to only about eighty-five hundred men, while Curtis had gathered a force of over twenty thousand, including Kansas militia as well as regular Federal soldiers. Nevertheless, Price decided to attack Curtis's army before Pleasonton could reach the scene. On the morning of October 23 at Westport (now part of Kansas City), Shelby's and Fagan's divisions launched a desperate battle with Curtis, while Marmaduke, contesting Pleasonton's crossing of the Big Blue River at Bryan's Ford, guarded their rear. The Battle of Westport, which some have called the Gettysburg of the West, raged all morning with about equal casualties on each side, but Price was obliged to retire when Pleasonton began to force a crossing of the river.

Some of the retreating Confederates, in their haste, abandoned muskets and other equipment on the field, but Shelby's division held off the Federals long enough for Price and the rest of the command to start south along the Kansas-Missouri border with the Confederate wagon train. The Federals did not immediately press their advantage, allowing the Confederates to march unmolested twenty-four miles and camp that evening on the Middle Fork of the Grand River. The next day, Price crossed into Kansas, marched south on the Fort Scott Road, and stopped for the evening near the small village of Trading Post on the Marais des Cygnes River.

On the morning of October 24, General Curtis, by seniority of rank, took command of the combined Federal forces and organized them into

PRICE'S 1864 INVASION
OF MISSOURI

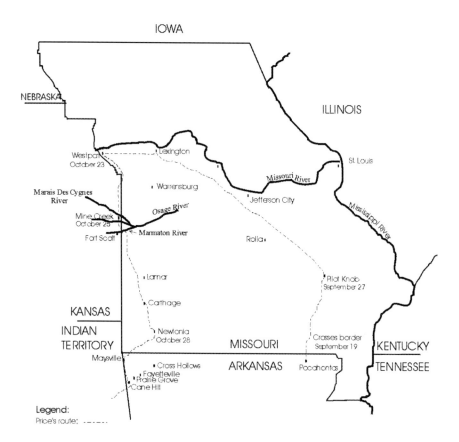

the Army of the Border. After sending most of the militia home, he gave General Blunt command of the regular troops from the Department of Kansas, which included soldiers from Colorado and Wisconsin, as well as Kansas, and designated them the First Division. Pleasonton's command, comprising Missouri, Arkansas, Iowa, and Indiana troops, was designated the Second Division.

The chase after Price then resumed and continued throughout the day. The Federals found the trail they were following strewn with abandoned equipment, exhausted animals, and deserters from the Rebel army. The Union advance caught up with Price's rear about midnight on the night of the twenty-fourth, encountering the Confederate pickets just north of Trading Post.

Early the next morning, the Federals launched an attack that drove the Rebels from their position and put them to flight. The bluecoats chased the fleeing Confederates across more than twenty miles of prairie in a running fight that lasted all day, engaging and routing them at the Marais des Cygnes, Mine Creek, and Shiloh Creek. In the most significant of the actions, the Battle of Mine Creek, General Marmaduke, General William L. Cabell (Fagan's second in command), several other officers, about five hundred enlisted men, and most of the Confederate cannons were captured. Total loss in killed, wounded, and captured was over one thousand, while the Federals suffered only about one hundred casualties.

On the night of October 25, the tired and dispirited Confederates paused to rest after crossing the Marmaton River, about eight miles east of Fort Scott, and Price tried to form his disheartened soldiers into some semblance of military order. Here also, finally convinced that the supply train he had sacrificed so much to save was only slowing him down, he destroyed some of the wagons and blew up the ammunition of the artillery guns that had fallen into enemy hands. Then his ragged army moved off toward Carthage in the middle of the night, while many of the Federals, particularly those of Pleasonton's command, retired to Fort Scott in search of food and rest.

Chapter 11

The Second Battle of Newtonia

G eneral Blunt's prestige had suffered greatly after his one-hundred-man escort was virtually annihilated by Quantrill's guerrillas at Baxter Springs in the fall of 1863, and at the beginning of the Confederate invasion of Missouri, he had been operating against Indians in the West with only a battalion-sized command. Eager to repair his tarnished reputation, Blunt started in pursuit of Price's retreating army on the late morning of October 26 with portions of the First, Second, and Fourth Brigades of his division. He struck the Confederates' trail at Shanghai, Missouri, near the Vernon-Barton county line, but camped there for the night.

Meanwhile, Price's exhausted army, with an eight-hour head start, pushed on throughout the morning and afternoon of the twenty-sixth toward Carthage because it was the nearest location where forage was readily available. The Southerners finally reached Carthage about nine o'clock that night after a march that lasted nineteen hours and covered almost sixty miles. Most of the men had gone without food all day, and it was eleven o'clock before they finally got supper. Dr. William M. McPheeters, a Confederate surgeon accompanying the march, wrote in his diary that it was 1:00 a.m. before he got to bed, but he "slept soundly when I got at it."

The next morning, October 27, General Blunt got an early start and was closing in on the Confederates camped at Carthage. At the same time,

Brigadier General John McNeil and Brigadier General Sanborn, with the Second and Third Brigades of Pleasonton's division, marched out of Fort Scott to join Blunt in the chase, while Pleasonton, who felt that there was little to gain by continuing the pursuit after Price's defeated army, retired to Warrensburg, Missouri, under escort.

Along the road near Lamar, Blunt came upon three members of the Kansas State Militia who had been Confederate prisoners but had escaped from Price the day before. "They were nearly starved," said an unidentified *Leavenworth Daily Conservative* correspondent, "having been prisoners five days and had had but two meals in the time; otherwise they had been well treated."

Meanwhile, the Confederates arose late at Carthage after their long, tiring trip the day before, and Price gave his soldiers time to eat breakfast. By the time the men were in the saddle and ready to take up the line of march toward Granby, it was almost eleven o'clock in the morning. Before leaving, Price decided that something needed to be done with the remaining Federal prisoners he had with him to keep them from slowing down the march. "Out of humanity," according to Price, the captives were paroled. The Confederates also left behind some of their own sick and starving men.

About 1:30 p.m., Blunt reached Carthage, where he found the paroled Federal soldiers and the ailing Confederates, one or two of whom had already died. Blunt's advance continued beyond Carthage and went into camp about five miles south of town just as the last of Price's stragglers were disappearing from view to the south.

After the Confederate march to Granby began, it encountered unexpected problems. A number of desertions took place among new recruits and the Arkansas troops (mostly attached to Fagan's division). Then the march was delayed when the Confederates met unusual difficulty fording a small millrace. Brigadier General M. Jeff Thompson, who brought up the rear of the march in command of Shelby's brigade of Shelby's division, still remembered the scene vividly years after the war. General Shelby, according to Thompson, "cursed himself hoarse" trying to goad the men and horses of his command across the creek. Thompson continued:

> *The multitude that had crossed this little stream had worn the banks*
> *perpendicular and muddied the water so that each horse stepped reluctantly*

General M. Jeff Thompson. *Courtesy of J. Dale West.*

into it or refused to move until spurred...The water was not six feet wide and one foot deep, but, as each file lost from one to five seconds, and we had five thousand files, more than two hours would be lost by such an obstacle, or the head of the column would gain six miles on the rear, while the rear had to recover by speed, or the front wait for them to close up. As we were all hungry and in sight of our camp fires, this was the more irritating, for each fellow when in the water felt safe and would try to water his horse, to the delay of those behind him.

About dark, the Confederates finally reached Shoal Creek just north of Granby, where they went into camp. Despite the difficulties they had encountered during the day's twenty-two-mile march, their spirits had improved somewhat because they had seen no sign of the pursuing Federals. The next morning, Shelby's brigade moved to the front and led the Confederate march across Shoal Creek, through Granby, and down the Newtonia road.

Meanwhile, the Federals broke camp early at Carthage and once again took up the chase, with Colonel James H. Ford, commanding Blunt's Fourth Brigade, in advance. About 10:00 a.m., Ford's advance came up on a rear guard of Price's command still in the woods north of Shoal Creek, having not yet crossed the stream. Ford sent two companies of Major James Ketner's Sixteenth Kansas Cavalry into the woods as skirmishers, and they soon returned with information that the Confederate party was only about two hundred strong and was rapidly retreating. Ford hurried forward and, upon reaching Granby, learned that the party he was pursuing had just passed through and that Price's whole army was at or en route to Newtonia, only five or six miles distant. The Fourth Brigade, which included Ford's Second Colorado Cavalry under the immediate command of Major Jesse L. Pritchard and Captain William D. McLain's First Colorado Battery, in addition to the Sixteenth Kansas, pressed on after the flying Rebels.

As Shelby's brigade approached Newtonia at midmorning, General Thompson learned from some of his men who were from the area that the town had a small Federal fort. He determined to attack and capture it by sending one advance party along the main road through town while another circled to the left to try to cut off a retreat. There was no need for reconnaissance, according to Thompson, since nearly every man in his brigade had fought at the first Newtonia battle and knew the ground well.

Because the town was located in an open prairie, however, it was almost impossible to maintain an element of surprise. By the time the Confederates reached the elevation northwest of Newtonia, they had been discovered, and "there was a stampede already going on." The two advance parties charged the fleeing Federals in what Thompson called "another steeplechase of life and death," and the party that took the left caught up with Lieutenant Christian, who had been the last to leave the fort, a couple of miles east of town.

According to Thompson, a young man whose father Christian had killed was among the pursuing party, and, taking the lead, he shot the lieutenant

Lieutenant Christian's grave at Newtonia Cemetery.

to death and mutilated his body before any officer could reach the scene. Another version of the story identifies the Confederate soldier who killed Christian as Samuel Moore and says that he galloped up and shot the lieutenant after he had already been taken prisoner. Perhaps the most thorough account of Christian's death appeared in a Springfield newspaper less than a year after the incident, but it said only that Christian was killed by a "gang of bushwhackers" who were acquainted with him. After killing him, the gang scalped him and hacked off part of his left hand. Returning to town with shouts and oaths, they displayed the bloody trophies to the Union ladies they met. A group of women from Newtonia that included Mathew Ritchey's daughter, Amanda, then went out, amid taunts from the Rebel soldiers, to retrieve Christian's body and brought it back to his home at the edge of town after the Second Battle of Newtonia had already begun raging nearby. Mary Grabill, who might otherwise have been among the party of women who retrieved the lieutenant's body, had, upon first learning in August of Price's rumored invasion of Missouri, left Newtonia with her family for an extended visit in Pennsylvania.

Trailing the two advance parties into Newtonia, Thompson and the rest of his men quickly took over the vacated fort, and the brigade commissary began issuing the rations found there. When the main body of Confederates started arriving shortly afterward, Thompson was ordered into camp at the timber three miles south of town with the rest of Price's army. Leaving a detachment under Lieutenant Colonel William H. Erwin to guard the Cassville road on the east side of town, Thompson retreated southward along the Pineville road and stopped at the edge of the woods, while the rest of the army, passing Shelby's brigade, continued farther south and camped near the Big Springs location that the Confederates had used during the First Battle of Newtonia. In addition to the picket under Erwin, a garrison of observation was also left at Newtonia to watch the Neosho, Granby, and Sarcoxie roads and to get the mill running.

Thompson and his men had been in camp a couple of hours when a Confederate scout rode in and announced that a body of Federals was very near. Shelby ordered Thompson to march the brigade on foot out onto the prairie and form in a line behind a new rail fence running along the south side of two adjacent fields about a half mile north of the timber. Unconvinced that the Yankees were at hand, the tired and hungry soldiers balked at the task, and Thompson could muster only about two hundred who were ready and willing to accompany him on the mission. Feeling that he had no time to lose, he hurried out with the available volunteers without taking time to gather more. Thompson and his men took up their position behind the fence and waited quite some time with no sign of the enemy. While they were there, several Confederate stragglers came down a nearby road and said that the report of Federals close at hand was entirely false. The detachment was soon afterward called back to camp.

The Federal pursuers had marched about halfway from Granby to Newtonia when the advance scouts, at about 2:00 p.m., spotted several stragglers at the rear of the Confederate march in the distance ahead. A courier raced back to report the news to Colonel Ford, who "hurried forward at a gallop." When he reached the top of the ridge about a mile northwest of Newtonia, he saw a number of Rebel camps and wagons at the edge of the woods two or three miles to his southeast, and the last of the Confederate train, retreating along the Pineville road, was entering the woods. A scattering

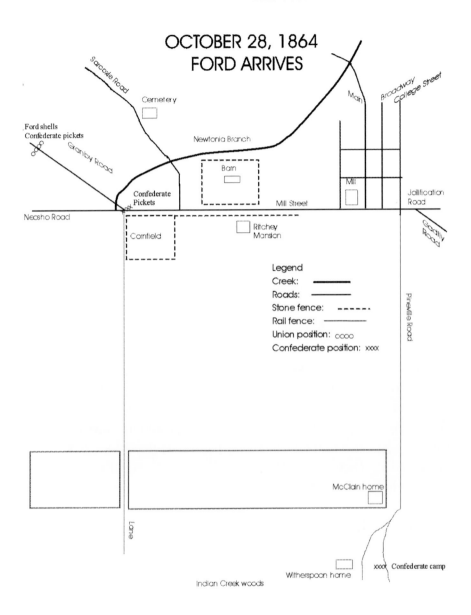

OCTOBER 28, 1864
FORD ARRIVES

Sarcoxie Road

Cemetery

Ford shells
Confederate pickets

Granby Road

Newtonia Branch

Main

Broadway

College Street

Barn

Mill

Jollification
Road

Confederate
Pickets

Mill Street

Neosho Road

Ritchey
Mansion

Cornfield

Gadfly
Road

Legend
Creek: ━━━━━
Roads: ─────
Stone fence: ------
Rail fence: ─────
Union position: oooo
Confederate position: xxxx

Pineville Road

McClain home

Lane

xxxx Confederate camp

Witherspoon home

Indian Creek woods

of Southern troops was swarming throughout the town, and smoke rising above the steam flouring mill suggested that the Confederates had it already up and running to supply their army with breadstuffs.

Seeing the bluecoats on the eminence overlooking Newtonia, the troops that occupied the village and the pickets guarding the western approaches to the town formed at the edge of the prairie west of town just beyond Ritchey's cornfield to meet the Federal advance. Ford promptly posted Captain McLain's battery on the ridge, formed the Second Colorado and the Sixteenth Kansas in two lines to support the artillery, and "commenced throwing shell" toward the Confederate skirmish line.

After the battery opened fire, General Blunt came up almost immediately to direct the battle. Thinking that the force opposing him was just a rear guard and that the Second Brigade of his division under Colonel Thomas Moonlight and Sanborn's and McNeil's brigades of Pleasonton's division would soon come up to reinforce him, Blunt ordered a charge. Under cover of the artillery, the Federal line, with the Sixteenth Kansas on the left and the Second Colorado on the right, started down the ridge, driving the skirmishers in a southwesterly direction across the prairie toward their camps in the timber over two miles away. With Blunt waving a revolver and leading the charge, the Federals left the road and, flanking the cornfield, gave pursuit.

Word passed quickly back through the Federal ranks that the advance had overtaken the Confederates and a skirmish was underway. The First Brigade raced forward at a trot to reinforce the Fourth. Commanded in the absence of Colonel Charles R. "Doc" Jennison by Lieutenant Colonel George H. Hoyt, the First Brigade consisted of Jennison's Fifteenth Kansas Cavalry, a battalion of the Third Wisconsin Cavalry under Lieutenant James Pond, and a section of howitzers under Sergeant George Patterson of the Fourteenth Kansas Cavalry. Hoyt's men trailed so closely on the heels of the Fourth Brigade that they were forced to gallop through "almost impenetrable clouds of dust" stirred up by the hurried march of Ford's command.

Arriving on the scene after Blunt had already begun his advance, the First Brigade, including Patterson's howitzers, dashed forward to join the march across the prairie toward the Confederate camps. The Fifteenth Kansas and Patterson's howitzers took up a position on the right of the Federal line, and Pond's Wisconsin battalion formed to the left of the Second Colorado Cavalry. Meanwhile, the First Colorado Battery continued to command the ridge northwest of town. Blunt's total force, consisting of two fragmented brigades, now totaled between nine hundred and one thousand men.

Returning to camp after going out under the false alarm, the Confederates had scarcely resumed their ordinary duties and pastimes when they heard the

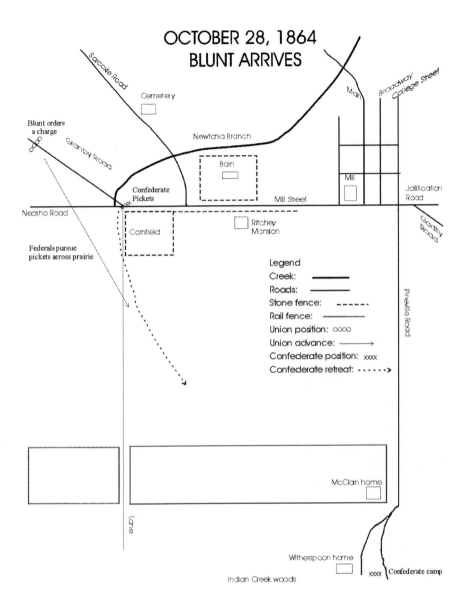

OCTOBER 28, 1864
BLUNT ARRIVES

Legend
Creek:
Roads:
Stone fence:
Rail fence:
Union position: oooo
Union advance: ⟶
Confederate position: xxxx
Confederate retreat: ••••••>

boom of Federal guns. Almost immediately, the pickets came rushing in with the news that the Yankees were advancing across the prairie. When Shelby again ordered his division out to meet them, this time the Southerners knew that it was no false alarm and turned out on the double. Emerging from the woods, they saw the Federals approaching the rail fence on the opposite side of the two fields, and the dismounted Confederates sprinted across the prairie to try to reach the fence at the south end of the field by the time the bluecoats got into position behind the corresponding fence on the north side.

A small lane running north and south separated the two fields, and Thompson's men took up position commanding the lane and immediately east of it. Lieutenant Colonel Alonzo W. Slayback's battalion, detached from Shelby's brigade, was stationed just to the west of the lane on Thompson's left, and Colonel Sidney D. Jackman's brigade held the right. A detachment under Major George Gordon (of Colonel B. Frank Gordon's regiment, Shelby's brigade) took up a position on the far left beside Slayback. Two mounted companies under Captains Maurice M. Langhorne and R.H. Adams, also detached from Shelby's brigade, occupied the extreme right of the line, and another small body of horsemen held the extreme left. These two detachments were the only Confederate soldiers on horseback except for three or four of the commanding officers. (The third brigade of Shelby's division, commanded by Colonel Charles H. Tyler, was incomplete, and many of the troops composing it were unarmed recruits.)

Both sides brought up their artillery as soon as they neared or reached the fences enclosing the fields. The Federal battery under Captain McLain rumbled down from the elevation and unlimbered at the center of the Federal line, while Shelby sent up two pieces of the Missouri Battery that had served him well at First Newtonia under Joe Bledsoe. Now commanded by Captain Richard A. Collins, the battery took up a position on the Confederate right, protected by Jackman's brigade.

Both sides attained the rail fences at about the same time, and, in the words the *Leavenworth Conservative* correspondent, "the battle opened fierce and furious." At first, it was strictly an artillery duel. Small-arms fire was reserved as the combatants faced one another at least five hundred yards distant from opposite sides of the enclosed fields, but the artillery of the two armies boomed away at each other. The Federals had two sections of big guns and one section of howitzers, while the Confederates had only Collins's two-gun battery, but, according to the correspondent to the Leavenworth newspaper, "their range was better than ours."

The Confederate shells "exploded in most dangerous proximity," while Captain McLain's Parrott rifles overshot their mark. The shells of the

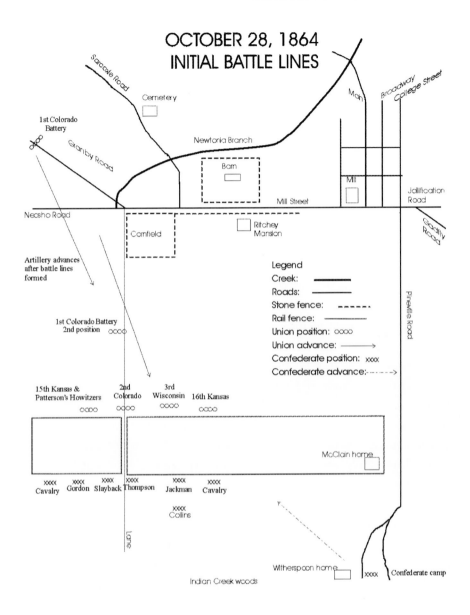

OCTOBER 28, 1864
INITIAL BATTLE LINES

Colorado battery tore through the trees south of the Confederate position and did minor damage to that part of Price's army that was still congregated in the woods but had little effect on the Rebels directly to the front. It was left to Patterson's light artillery to answer the Confederate guns, and the opposing batteries fought to a virtual draw for some time.

The two fields enclosed by the rail fences were part of the Thomas McClain farm, and the fence on the south side extended east to McClain's brick home located along the Pineville road. Shortly after the battle began, the home was pressed into service as a field hospital to treat the Confederate wounded, and the Rebels raised a yellow flag atop the house so that it wouldn't be shelled. The Witherspoon home slightly south of the McClain place was also reportedly used as a field hospital by the Southerners.

As the battle raged, Thompson sent messengers to Shelby and Price requesting reinforcements, but none were forthcoming. Price had already started his wagons and most of the rest of his army south at the first sound of the Federal guns. It hardly mattered anyway because Shelby's brigade was the only effective fighting force left in Price's army. On more than one occasion during the Confederate retreat southward along the Kansas-Missouri border, Shelby's brigade had saved the Rebels from utter annihilation, earning along the way a reputation as the "Iron Brigade" for the unbending resolve of its men, and once again the brigade was called upon to cover the Rebel withdrawal, buying time for Price's army to get farther south.

When the accuracy of Collins's gunners finally began to soften up the Federal line, Thompson ordered a charge. His men promptly leaped the rail fence and started across the field toward the Federals, while Jackman's brigade stayed behind to protect the battery. Even though Thompson pressed forward with only Shelby's brigade, and the ranks of that unit had been thinned, the Confederate force still outnumbered the Federals who faced them. Opening fire with small arms when they were within range, the Rebels began gradually pushing the Northerners back. Thompson passed up the lane between the two fields on horseback, staying even with the Confederate line and "directing the men to keep cool and go slow."

The Federal line had fallen back several hundred yards by the time the Confederates reached the field's north fence, and after only a moment's pause, the grayclads jumped the second fence and resumed their steady march across the open prairie. Colonel Moses W. Smith of the Eleventh Missouri Cavalry was shot through the thigh and mortally wounded as he stood on the rail fence cheering his men on.

The dismounted Confederates could not effectively charge the mounted Federals, but they slowly pushed them back with their superior numbers.

Extending their line, the Rebels threatened to flank the Federal right, but a galling fire from Patterson's howitzers checked the movement. The Confederates momentarily fell back, and it was with difficulty that the Rebel commanders goaded their men into renewing the attack.

Soon, however, the long Confederate line was once again threatening the Federal flanks, and Blunt ordered the Colorado battery to fall back about five hundred yards and take up a position near Ritchey's cornfield. The rest of the Federal line was also instructed to fall back slowly and re-form in support of the battery, but the alacrity with which McLain carried out his orders caused panic among the Federal ranks. Seeing the horses of the Colorado battery galloping to the rear, some of the men from the Fifteenth and Sixteenth Kansas Cavalries started stampeding toward the rear as well. The Confederates pressed forward with renewed vigor when they saw the retreat. The Federal officers, by utmost exertion, finally stayed the stragglers as McLain's artillery came into battery, and Blunt re-formed his line "in the face of a terrific fire." A few hurried rounds from the Colorado guns not only halted the Southern advance but also once again drove the Confederates back, as the two sides, in the words of General Curtis, moved "forward and back alternately."

A Second Colorado trooper's colorful and, no doubt, embellished account of the Newtonia battle, penned a few months after the fact, suggests the seesaw nature of the engagement:

> *The rebels had planted a battery in their rear, that was throwing shell with considerable precision into the midst of our troops, but notwithstanding the fierce storm of leaden hail from the enemy's guns, that thinned our ranks, and stilled the pulsations of many a noble heart—they stood, firm and undaunted; and when the order to fire was given, the long line of curling smoke, the rattling, cracking, crashing of the carbines in the hands of our men, that hurled leaden messengers of death into the ranks of the foe, and the deep thunder tones of our batteries, that belched forth shot and shell—spake full many a traitor's doom, and served to check their impetuous advance, and cause them to fall back in confusion, but only to return to the charge with increased numbers, and greater determination. At half past four o'clock, the battle was raging in all its fury. The inspiring cheers of the combatants, the*

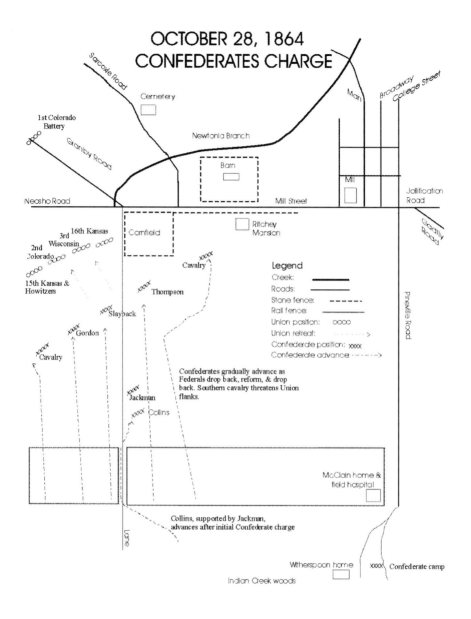

OCTOBER 28, 1864
CONFEDERATES CHARGE

Sarcoxie Road

Cemetery

Man

Broadway College Street

1st Colorado Battery

Granby Road

Newtonia Branch

Barn

Mill

Neosho Road

Mill Street

Jollification Road

Godfry Road

3rd 16th Kansas
2nd Wisconsin
Colorado

Cornfield

Ritchey Mansion

Cavalry

15th Kansas & Howitzers

Thompson

Legend

Creek:
Roads:
Stone fence: - - - - -
Rail fence:
Union position: oooo
Union retreat: · · · · · · >
Confederate position: xxxx
Confederate advance: · — · — · >

Slayback

Gordon

Cavalry

Confederates gradually advance as Federals drop back, reform, & drop back. Southern cavalry threatens Union flanks.

Jackman

Collins

Pineville Road

McClain home & field hospital

Collins, supported by Jackman, advances after initial Confederate charge

Lane

Witherspoon home

xxxx Confederate camp

Indian Creek woods

constant roar of artillery; and the incessant rattle of fire-arms, that dealt death and destruction on either side; the clashing of sabres, mingled with the death-cries of the fallen, and the shouts of the officers in giving commands; the galloping to and fro of couriers carrying orders—all tended to make the scene one of thrilling interest, and exciting in the extreme.

Regrouping, the Confederates threw out a large force on the Federal left and began to press forward yet again, "their fire telling fearfully upon our small force," according to Colonel Ford. Some of the men of the Fifteenth and Sixteenth Kansas Cavalries began to exhaust their ammunition because Blunt's hurried chase after Price had outrun the ammunition train. Still, claimed Colonel Hoyt, the Kansans stood "under fire a long time without a cartridge to return the galling fire of the enemy."

It was nearing sundown, and the Rebel force on the Federal left was threatening a flanking movement around and through Ritchey's cornfield that could completely encircle the Federals. Blunt was running low on ammunition and was unable to extend his small line to meet the Confederate threat. He instructed the Colorado battery to fall back to the foot of the ridge northwest of town and was about to order a general retreat when General Sanborn, with Pleasonton's Third Brigade, appeared atop the ridge.

Arriving with Sanborn's brigade, General Curtis saw some of the Federal troops "hard pressed and giving way. McLain's battery, badly cut up, was falling back for safety," and a number of stragglers, some of them wounded, were retreating without orders. As Sanborn hurried forward to reinforce Blunt, McLain, under Curtis's direction, immediately turned his guns on the Confederates. Seeing the fortunate turn of events, the slackers faced about and dashed back to the field with a shout.

Blunt immediately placed Sanborn's brigade on his left with orders to advance through the cornfield to meet the Confederate flanking column. Because the field, like much of Mathew Ritchey's estate, was surrounded by stone walls, Sanborn was obliged to dismount his troops, and they were ordered forward "as fast as they could dismount and form."

With the Sixth Cavalry Missouri State Militia and the Second Arkansas Cavalry leading the way, Sanborn's brigade advanced steadily through the field, and the Federal right, reinvigorated by the timely arrival of reinforcements, also pressed forward. At the same time, a section of artillery under Captain William C.F. Montgomery of the Second Missouri Light Artillery that was attached to Sanborn's command unlimbered and opened fire on the Confederate center, firing twenty-two rounds in all.

General Thompson had brought up his battery to support his line as it advanced across the prairie, but now, as the bluecoats marched forward, he

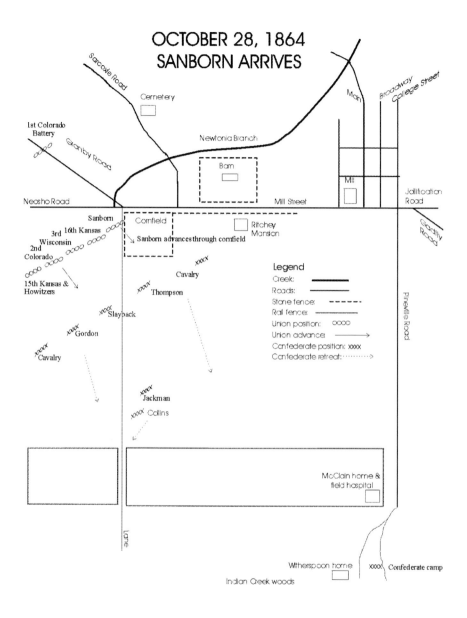

OCTOBER 28, 1864
SANBORN ARRIVES

Sarcoxie Road

Cemetery

1st Colorado Battery

Granby Road

Newtonia Branch

Barn

Man

Broadway

College Street

Mill

Jollification Road

Goathy Road

Neosho Road

Mill Street

Sanborn

Cornfield

3rd 16th Kansas

2nd Wisconsin

Colorado

Sanborn advances through cornfield

Ritchey Mansion

15th Kansas & Howitzers

Cavalry

Thompson

Slayback

Gordon

Cavalry

Jackman

Collins

McClain home & field hospital

Witherspoon home

Confederate camp

Indian Creek woods

Lane

Pineville Road

Legend

Creek:	——
Roads:	——
Stone fence:	- - - -
Rail fence:	—·—·—
Union position:	○○○○
Union advance:	——→
Confederate position:	xxxx
Confederate retreat:	········>

withdrew the artillery. When the Federal advance got to within range and fired two or three volleys in quick succession, the Confederate cavalry also began to retire, and a jubilant cheer went up among the Federal ranks. A detachment of troops from Fagan's division finally arrived on the field about this time, but the Southern reinforcements were too late, as the Rebels were already retreating

Cornfield through which Sanborn advanced as it appears today. The Ritchey Mansion is in the background.

toward the Indian Creek woods. The rejuvenated Federal line pursued them for some distance across the prairie before calling off the chase.

According to Colonel John E. Phelps, commanding the Second Arkansas, the retreating Confederates were "heedless of the bugle that called to the charge," but Thompson suggested that he had ordered a withdrawal even before the Federal reinforcements made their appearance—as soon as Blunt began retiring from his last position. Given the weariness of the troops on both sides and the approach of darkness, it is probably safe to say that neither the Federals nor the Confederates were eager to prolong the contest.

Both sides, however, claimed victory at Second Newtonia. Phelps, for instance, suggested that the timely arrival of Sanborn's brigade had "turned a defeat into a victory." On the other hand, Shelby (or rather his chief of staff, Major John N. Edwards, who wrote all of Shelby's battle reports at this stage of the war) claimed, "Night closed the contest, and another beautiful victory had crowned the Confederate arms."

Despite such Confederate declarations of victory, the fact remains that, in the words of Phelps, the Southerners "left the historical field of Newtonia in Federal hands," abandoning their dead and gravely wounded. Thus, even though Shelby had accomplished his purpose of stalling the Federal pursuit long enough to let the rest of Price's army move off unmolested, the Second Battle of Newtonia is considered a Union victory.

The Federals stayed on the battlefield until about 9:00 p.m., at which time they retired to Newtonia to spend the night. Meanwhile, Shelby lingered in the woods south of town until about midnight. Then, leaving a detachment under Colonel Erwin to watch the Federal movements, he retired along the Pineville road to try to catch up with the rest of the Confederate train. After standing guard throughout the night, Erwin also started south early the next morning.

During and after the battle, the Federals removed their wounded to some of the homes, including the Ritchey Mansion, in Newtonia, where they were reportedly well cared for by the women of the town. The next day, some of the seriously wounded were taken to Mount Vernon. After the Confederate retreat, the Southern wounded at the McClain and Witherspoon homes also fell into Federal hands. Many of the dead from both sides were buried at the cemetery just north of Newtonia, although most of the Union dead, excluding Lieutenant Christian, were reinterred at the National Cemetery in Springfield a few years later.

The number of casualties at Second Newtonia was about equal on both sides. Some estimates have placed the total as high as 650 (400 Union and 250 Confederate), but this is almost surely a vast overstatement.

Blunt, whose command sustained virtually all of the Federal casualties at Newtonia, stated in the official report of his operations against Price, written in December 1864, that one-eighth of his force that was engaged at Newtonia was either killed or wounded. However, his total force engaged, according to several different sources, numbered slightly over 900. In a letter to General James H. Lane written two days after the battle, Blunt placed his total casualties at 118. This generally agrees with the figure suggested by an anonymous *Leavenworth Conservative* correspondent who filed a report the day after the battle. He gave precise figures for each of Blunt's units engaged in the fight and listed Blunt's aggregate losses at 18 killed, 95 wounded, and 1 missing, for total casualties of 114. Of the wounded, not more than 20 were seriously hurt, according to the correspondent. (This correspondent was probably Captain Richard Josiah Hinton, an aide to Blunt who wrote a book the next year about the Federal campaign against Price. If Hinton was not the newspaper correspondent, he borrowed from the correspondent's report almost word for word when he wrote his book.) In addition to the casualties among the troops, the Federals also lost over one hundred horses killed or wounded.

None of the Confederate officers who filed official reports pertaining to the Second Battle of Newtonia gave any indication of their number of casualties. Dr. McPheeters mentioned in his late-night diary entry of October 28 that earlier that evening he had attended to 24 or 25 men and officers at the Confederate field hospital. (He didn't indicate that there was more than one hospital, and there probably was only one primary one—the McClain home.) A Union spy who was with the Confederates prior to and during the Newtonia battle came into the Federal camp the day after the battle and reported the number of Rebels wounded at 175, 35 of whom were injured seriously enough to require hospitalization. Blunt, in his letter to General Lane, claimed that a Confederate surgeon who came into the Federal lines under a flag of truce to ask for morphine placed the total number of Southern casualties, including killed and wounded, at over 200. Both of these Federal estimates of Confederate losses at Newtonia may be somewhat high, just as Union officials' estimates of their own losses may be slightly low, since each side during the Civil War tended to exaggerate the losses of the enemy and minimize its own. However, it is fairly safe to say that the total losses for both sides at the Second Battle of Newtonia did not approach 650 and may not have reached half that number.

After the Second Battle of Newtonia, General Blunt was alternately praised for his heroics in almost single-handedly defeating the Confederates or criticized for his haste in rushing forward before reinforcements could come up and thereby risking annihilation. The Leavenworth newspaper correspondent, for instance, claimed that Blunt deserved "great credit for his coolness, courage and usefulness." A postwar detractor, on the other hand, said that Blunt's rashness in "rushing ahead with two small brigades of less than two regiments in number to attack the Confederate army after it had rested and to some extent reorganized would hardly have been excusable in a captain commanding a company, much less in a major-general commanding a division." Despite his critics, Blunt's campaign against Price at Little Blue, at Westport, and now at Newtonia would, in the end, go a long way toward restoring the prestige he had lost at Baxter Springs the previous year.

Chapter 12

Price's Retreat and the End of the War in Missouri

Planning to resume the pursuit of the Confederates early the next morning in hopes of crushing Price's demoralized army, General Curtis allowed his men a brief rest at Newtonia after the battle of October 28. He gave orders for the Federals to be ready to ride at 3:00 a.m., but just as they were falling out in the early morning darkness to form for the march, a runner from Fort Scott galloped in carrying a telegraph message that General Pleasonton had wired from Warrensburg. The dispatch announced orders from General Rosecrans, dated October 27, directing the withdrawal of all of Pleasonton's troops, including Sanborn's and McNeil's brigades.

General Curtis was "astonished and sorely disappointed" by General Rosecrans's order, which had been issued based on the representations of General Pleasonton that Price's army had been completely defeated and that further pursuit was unnecessary. There had been friction between Pleasonton and Curtis almost from the time their two divisions were thrown together as the Army of the Border for the campaign against Price. A particular sore spot among Pleasonton's troops was the fact that Curtis had issued an order at Mine Creek directing that any prisoners or trophies of battle taken in Kansas were to remain in Kansas, and many of Pleasonton's officers and men had determined not to serve under Curtis any longer than was absolutely necessary to drive Price into Arkansas.

Thus, at daylight on October 29, General Sanborn started for Springfield to resume command of the Southwest District. General McNeil, who had arrived at Newtonia the previous evening after the battle was over, accompanied Sanborn to Springfield with plans to continue to his district headquarters at Rolla. The departures left Curtis with only General Blunt's fragmented division, fewer than one thousand strong. Curtis sent a dispatch by courier to Cassville, where the nearest telegraph station was located, to be wired to General Henry W. Halleck, chief of staff of the Union army, apprising him of Pleasonton's withdrawal.

Then, unable to resume the pursuit of Price with his own small force, Curtis retired grudgingly toward Kansas and camped on the evening of the twenty-ninth at Neosho, ten miles west of Newtonia. At midnight, however, a messenger reached Neosho carrying a dispatch from Halleck informing Curtis that Lieutenant General Ulysses S. Grant, commanding the Union army, desired that Price be pursued to the Arkansas River or at least until he encountered the Army of Arkansas (Union) under Generals Frederick Steele and Joseph J. Reynolds.

The message from Halleck, dated October 28 (the day before Curtis's wire to Halleck), clearly countermanded, at least in Curtis's mind, the order from General Rosecrans. "Much and agreeably surprised" to receive the dispatch from Halleck, Curtis immediately sent orders by courier to the retiring brigades directing Generals Sanborn and McNeil, as well as Pleasonton's other brigade commanders (Colonel John F. Phillips and Lieutenant Colonel Frederick W. Benteen), to "proceed forthwith to Cassville" and report to Curtis at that point. He also dispatched a courier with a message to be telegraphed to Rosecrans informing the general of the actions he had taken and the authority by which he had taken them. Then, on the early morning of October 30, he set out for Cassville under the false belief that Price had retreated in that direction, and he camped that night at Newtonia.

The next day, Curtis marched as far as Gadfly, where he learned that Price had retired by way of Pineville; so the Federals turned due south and camped near Keetsville on the evening of October 31. Curtis was purposely proceeding by short marches to allow time for the expected reinforcements under Sanborn and McNeil to catch up with him.

Those officers, however, were reluctant to respond to the orders recalling them to the field against Price. Curtis's courier carrying the orders had not reached the generals until they were very near Springfield, and, since they were so near, they had gone on to Springfield for rest and provisions. In addition, Sanborn, while at Springfield, was ordered by Rosecrans to take command of all the Department of the Missouri troops remaining in the Southwest District and to operate against Price with them, an order that effectively removed the Missouri troops from Curtis's Army of the Border. Sanborn nonetheless started belatedly toward Cassville about the first of November to reinforce Curtis, and Lieutenant Colonel Benteen, who was already in the Cassville vicinity, was directed to cooperate with Curtis as well. Commanding the Fourth Brigade of Pleasonton's division, Benteen made a juncture with Curtis at Keetsville on the morning of November 1. Meanwhile, McNeil declined to resume the campaign at all, claiming that his troops and horses were too exhausted from the previous marches.

After leaving Newtonia on the evening of October 28, Price retreated south by way of Pineville. During the march, the weather turned cold, and disease began to ravage Price's already exhausted, half-starved army. Many stragglers deserted for home or dropped by the wayside. On November 1, the spiritless army staggered into Cane Hill, Arkansas, where, having seen no sign of the pursuing Federals, Price paused to rest and gather supplies.

On the same day that Price reached Cane Hill, Curtis left Keetsville with Benteen's brigade and his own small force and arrived at Pea Ridge that evening. He remained at Pea Ridge the next day, futilely awaiting further reinforcements under Sanborn or McNeil, and then marched to Cross Hollows on November 3.

Soon after the Confederates reached Cane Hill, word arrived that Colonel William H. Brooks of the Thirty-fourth Arkansas Infantry was besieging the Federal garrison at Fayetteville, and General Fagan requested and received permission to aid in the attack. Borrowing two guns from Collins's battery and five hundred men from Shelby's division, which was the only real fighting force left, Fagan marched twenty miles to the northeast and joined in the attack at Fayetteville on November 3. His men, however, had so little enthusiasm for the job that they could scarcely be goaded into advancing within rifle range of the Federal defenders under Colonel Marcus LaRue Harrison.

Learning that Curtis was approaching from the north, Fagan returned to Cane Hill, where the disintegration of the Confederate army continued. Entire regiments and even brigades of Arkansas conscripts disbanded and headed for home. Virtually powerless to prevent the desertions, Price merely instructed his officers to try to collect the absentees during the month of December and bring them back into the Confederate lines at that time, if possible. Other units, including Jackman's brigade, were allowed to leave the army temporarily for the purpose of visiting friends and relatives.

On November 4, Price's demoralized army, consisting now of only four brigades and Tyler's recruits, left Cane Hill. Afraid of being intercepted if he tried to cross the Arkansas River between Little Rock and Fort Smith, Price marched west into Indian Territory and crossed the river on November 7 at a place known as Pheasant Ford about twenty-five miles from Fort Smith.

Learning after his arrival at Cross Hollows that the Federal garrison at Fayetteville was under siege, Curtis marched to the relief of Colonel Harrison early on the morning of November 4 and reached Fayetteville just as Fagan's rear guard was retreating. Reinforced by a detachment under Harrison, Curtis resumed his pursuit of Price on the fifth and camped that night at Prairie Grove. The next morning, the Federals passed through Cane Hill, where they took prisoner a number of sick and broken-down stragglers from Price's army and then paroled them. For the next two days, Curtis continued to hound Price's trail, finding abandoned animals and wagons along the way. On November 8, the Federals reached the timber of the Arkansas River and drove the last of the Confederate rear guard across the river. Bringing up his artillery, Curtis shelled the woods on the other side and then called off the chase. Declaring victory, he issued congratulatory orders disbanding the Army of the Frontier and telling his men, "The object of this organization and campaign is accomplished."

Price's great raid into Missouri, on the other hand, ended in utter failure. Continuing south, his wretched army reached Bonham, Texas, on November 23, where the men finally received full rations and their spirits lifted somewhat. From Bonham, Price moved eastward and established his headquarters at Laynesport, Arkansas.

At the outset of his mission, Price had hoped to take and hold Missouri, to attract vast numbers of recruits to his army, and even to be in a strong

Second Battle of Newtonia marker on the grounds of the Ritchey Mansion.

enough position to influence the outcome of the 1864 presidential election. Instead, he had been on the run almost from the time he entered Missouri in mid-September, and recruits had not flocked to him in the numbers he had envisioned. Most of those who had enlisted were unarmed, and many used his expedition as an excuse for plunder. Citizens of his home state had not rallied to him as he had hoped and expected, and if his raid had any effect on the election, it was the opposite effect from what he had intended. Confederate authorities tried to put the best possible face on the defeat by claiming that Price's invasion had kept occupied in Missouri thousands of Federal troops that might otherwise have reinforced General William Sherman in the East, but the result of the raid left Price himself bitterly disappointed.

The Second Battle of Newtonia would stand as the last significant engagement in Missouri. The Civil War in the state, after Price's raid, was reduced to occasional skirmishing and raiding by guerrilla bands.

Mary Grabill came home from Pennsylvania in January 1865 through bitter cold and snow, but as the war wound down, a semblance of normalcy gradually returned to Newtonia. Years later, Mary reflected on the war and wondered how she had lived through all the hardships it entailed:

> *In looking back over the terrible four years of wartime, a few bright spots loom out. There were some beautiful friendships growing out of the dark time, and memories come back of lovely evenings with cultured officers and their wives, who often bore them company—such people as we rarely met in our ordinary lives down here.*
>
> *We could not anticipate all the trouble that came—it was only day by day. And in the end, the relief of peace was saddened by the knowledge of the bitterness defeat brought to many beloved ones.*

Chapter 13

Battlefields Preservation and Newtonia Today

S ince the end of the war, various efforts have been undertaken to preserve and maintain the Newtonia cemetery where soldiers from both battles were buried, and the site is now commonly called the Civil War Cemetery. These maintenance efforts began shortly after the war's close, but they have been sporadic until recent years.

In 1868, most of the Union dead were removed from the cemetery and reinterred at the National Cemetery in Springfield. Ninety-four dollars in gold and ten dollars in silver were found in the pockets of one of the soldiers when his body was uncovered. Lieutenant Robert Christian was one of the few Union soldiers whose body was left at the Newtonia cemetery, and his grave is the only one with a stone identifying the occupant by name. According to oral tradition, many Confederates were also interred at Newtonia. The Civil War cemetery has numerous graves marked only by sandstones or field rocks, and presumably some of these unidentified graves belong to the Confederate dead.

In 1869, a Christmas festival was held at the college building in Newtonia to raise funds for fencing the cemetery, and almost four hundred people attended, "all of whom enjoyed themselves until the 'wee small hours,'" according to a report in a Neosho newspaper, "and withdrew, conscious of having aided a noble enterprise." The event raised about $150 for the fencing project.

Clearing the Newtonia Civil War Cemetery, 1961. *Courtesy of David Weems.*

In 1905, a Newtonia woman named Sarah Prater raised sixty-four dollars to have the cemetery cleaned up. She paid the workmen fifty dollars for the job and deposited the remainder in the Granby bank.

For many years during the early twentieth century, another local woman, Grandma Pierce, collected funds for the upkeep of the cemetery. After she died in 1940, no one volunteered to tend the cemetery, and over the next twenty years, it became overgrown with thick underbrush of sprouts, weeds, and vines.

In 1961, a Baptist minister from Rolla tried to visit the cemetery but found it so dense with undergrowth that he was unable to reach it. Returning to town, he borrowed some tools from local resident David Weems but was still unable to clear away enough brush to reach the cemetery. Later, Weems recruited a crew of local boys and cleared a path to the cemetery. Shortly afterward, several local citizens banded together and began an organized cleanup of the Civil War Cemetery, and since that time a concentrated effort has been made to maintain the burial ground.

In 1868, Newtonia suffered a major fire that destroyed most of the business district. Among the buildings destroyed was the Ritchey mill at the corner

Newtonia Civil War Cemetery today.

of Mill and Elm Streets, the same mill that had been pressed into service during the Civil War to supply breadstuffs for whichever side happened to be occupying the town at the time. A new mill to take the old one's place was constructed slightly west of and across the street from the Ritchey home.

One of the few structures in town to survive the 1868 fire was the Ritchey Mansion. Mathew Ritchey continued to live in the house until his death in 1889. (He also had a home at Ritchey, a small community north of Newtonia that was founded after the Civil War on land he donated, and the town was named after him.) His widow, Mary Eliza Clark Ritchey, stayed in the mansion until she died in 1895. Both she and Ritchey's first wife are buried alongside him at the family plot on the grounds of his Newtonia home. The house remained in the Ritchey family after Mrs. Ritchey's death. Mathew's daughter Margaret Eliza Ritchey Graves lived in it until 1937, when it passed to her daughter, Mildred Graves Sanders. The home finally left the Ritchey family in 1948, when it was sold to A.T. Irwin. Ralph and Louise Murphy acquired the house in 1950 and made a number of improvements to it. Robert R. and Margaret Ann Darch bought the home in 1961. It was

Mr. and Mrs. Ritchey, circa 1885. *Courtesy of Larry James.*

placed on the National Register of Historic Places in 1978. The nomination form cited the house's status as one of the oldest surviving homes in Newton County and its Civil War legacy, particularly the Belle Starr legend. The Ritchey Mansion stayed in the Darch family for another twenty years after it was placed on the National Register of Historic Places and then was sold to Tracy and Teresa Ledbetter in 1998.

The Ritchey barn, which the Confederates used as a fortification during the First Battle of Newtonia, also survived the fire, but it was dismantled sometime around the turn of the twentieth century. The stone fence on the Ritchey property was taken down about the same time as the barn. Many of

Ritchey family cemetery near the mansion.

the same stones were used to erect a similar fence along Highway 86 at the south edge of Newtonia when that road was built in the early 1900s. Even the "new" fence has now virtually disappeared.

Besides the mill, another business structure lost to the 1868 fire was the E.H. Grabill store. Early the next year, Grabill purchased from the Ritcheys the lot where the old mill had stood and erected a dry goods store at the location. In 1872, Grabill sold the business to A.J. Porter and Company. The Grabills still lived in Newtonia in 1880, and E.H. Grabill was listed on the census as a retired merchant. In 1882, the family moved to Springfield, where E.H. Grabill went into the banking business. He died at Springfield in 1909. Mary continued to live in Springfield, and it was sometime during her later years that she was prevailed upon by her daughters to record her memories of the war in the form of a letter to them. Mary Grabill died in 1912 and is buried at Maple Park Cemetery in Springfield.

Through the efforts of a committee that included Judge Paul Carver, Carroll Gum, and Charys Weems, a monument commemorating the two Newtonia battle sites was erected in 1961 and dedicated by Missouri governor

John Dalton during a ceremony on November 14 of that year. According to longtime Newtonia preservationist David Weems, erection of this monument was the first step toward memorializing the part that Newtonia played in the Civil War in Missouri. The marker sits on Highway 86 at a curve just east of the Newtonia turnoff. Most of the action on September 30, 1862, occurred north and northwest of the marker, in the town proper and beyond, while

Missouri governor John Dalton dedicates the Newtonia battles monument, 1961. *Courtesy of Larry James.*

the primary scene of battle on October 20, 1864, was west and southwest of the marker.

In 1993, the Civil War Sites Advisory Commission of the National Park Service designated the Newtonia battlefields among the top fifty most threatened battlefields in the country. The 1864 battlefield was placed on the Priority I list as one of the twenty-five most endangered battlefields, and the 1862 site was placed on the Priority II list among the top fifty most endangered. (The two sites overlap slightly, mainly at the southwest edge of town.)

In March 1994, the Newtonia Battlefields Protection Association was formed to preserve the Newtonia battlefields and promote the town's Civil War history. Founding members Tom Higdon, Larry James, and David Weems have served continuously on the board of the organization since its inception and are the only members to serve as president. Other people who are or have been active in the group include Kay and Russell Hively, Linda James, Gail Higdon, Ilene Garner, Joann Turner, Kristen Reber, Gail Elery, Charys Weems, Rusty Hively, Jerry Faules, Don Johnston, Don and Denise Jessen, John and Betty Wright, and Jim and Cathy Sheehy.

In 1996, the Newtonia Battlefields Protection Association acquired its first parcel of land that was part of the Newtonia battlefields when David and Charys Weems donated 8.3 acres to the group. The land is located north of the Ritchey Mansion within the boundaries of the first Newtonia battleground. In 2002, the association obtained a loan for almost $300,000 and purchased the Ritchey Mansion and 11.0 acres of land surrounding the home. The next year, the group received a federal grant for about half the purchase price to help repay the loan, and the rest of the debt was soon retired through donations. In 2004, the protection association obtained the Ritchey family cemetery. The group also tends the Civil War Cemetery so that, all together, the organization is owner or caretaker of about 25.0 acres of land that were part of the Newtonia battlefields.

In 1995, the Newtonia Battlefields Protection Association commissioned an assessment and archaeological survey of the two battlefields by Garrow and Associates of Atlanta. Results of the study were published in the form of a booklet entitled *Engaged the Enemy Again* by lead researcher Robert Fryman. In 1998, the group commissioned a second archaeological study, conducted

Ritchey Mansion, circa 2005, before tree removal.

by White Star Consulting of Mount Pleasant, Tennessee, in conjunction with the Battlefields Protection Program of the National Park Service. The results were published as *Newtonia Battlefields Archaeological Survey*. Then, in 2000, Gray and Pape of Cincinnati conducted a third study, also under the aegis of the Newtonia Battlefields Protection Association, for the purpose of formulating a preservation plan for the battlefields.

In 2001, the Civil War Preservation Trust, a nonprofit organization dedicated to preserving Civil War battle sites, listed the Newtonia battlefields among the twenty-five most endangered in the nation, reflecting the earlier designation by the Civil War Sites Advisory Commission.

In 2004, the Newtonia Battlefields Protection Association was instrumental in getting the two Newtonia battlefields added to the National Register of Historic Places as separate entities.

The organization had accomplished a lot in ten short years, but members envisioned much more—the Ritchey Mansion fully restored, a visitors' center, and driving tours of the battle sites. Some dared to dream of a day when their organization might not even be necessary, and their mission of preserving and protecting the Newtonia battlefields would be taken over by the federal government.

In 2006, U.S. Representative Roy Blunt introduced legislation in Congress to authorize a study of the feasibility of making the Newtonia battlefields part of the National Park Service, either as a branch of the Wilson's Creek National Battlefield Park or as a separate entity. Representing the Newtonia Battlefields Protection Association, Kay Hively testified before the House of Representatives on behalf of the legislation in September 2006. Although the House passed the legislation in late 2006, it was not considered by the Senate during that legislative session, and Representative Blunt reintroduced the legislation early the following year.

While the legislation was making its way through Congress, events related to the battlefields and the Ritchey Mansion continued to unfold back at Newtonia. In 2007, the Newtonia Battlefields Protection Association received a $10,000 donation from the Eastern Shawnee Tribe of Oklahoma and the Newton County Tourism Committee for the creation of a mural at the Ritchey Mansion centered on the theme of American Indian participation in the First Battle of Newtonia. Later, the association commissioned local artist Doug Hall to do the mural, and he is putting the finishing touches on the project as of this writing. Also in 2007, several large trees on the grounds of the mansion were removed after a severe ice storm in early 2007 did minor damage to the house. The following year, a tornado did extensive damage to the mansion, necessitating costly repair.

Meanwhile, the legislation authorizing the feasibility study of the Newtonia battlefields was passed by both houses of Congress and was signed into law by President George W. Bush in May 2008. It was not until late 2009, however, that funding for the study was finally approved and plans for its implementation announced. As of this writing, the study is scheduled to begin in 2010 and will take an estimated eighteen to twenty-four months to complete. (A film documentary about the battles of Newtonia is also scheduled for production during 2010.) Connie Langum, a historian at Wilson's Creek National Battlefield, has been commissioned to write the feasibility study's statement of significance, which will show why the Newtonia sites are important and unique among other Civil War sites in the National Park Service.

Ritchey Mansion today.

Ms. Hively, a founding member of the protection association, points out that the mere fact that a small community like Newtonia had two Civil War battles is in itself interesting and unique, and "each of those battles was significant." If the current feasibility study results in the Newtonia battlefields being placed under the umbrella of the National Park Service, Hively says that she will "rest knowing that the battlefields are in probably the best hands" and that the sites will continue to be well cared for, even after those individuals like herself, who have been instrumental in the Newtonia Battlefields Protection Association's efforts from the beginning, are gone.

Still very much a rural village, the town of Newtonia today is remarkably similar to the way it was, or at least the way one might imagine it was, during the Civil War. The basic pattern of streets is the same as it was when the town was laid out in the 1850s, with Mill Street being the main east–west street and College, Broadway, and Main Streets still forming the principal north–south streets. The population of the town has increased by only a little over one hundred people, and several of the roads just outside town are not paved. And if you listen closely, standing at the side of one of the undeveloped roads in the quiet of the prairie, you can still hear the echo of the cannons.

A Note on Maps and Troop Movements

As readers familiar with previous accounts of the First Battle of Newtonia may have noted, my maps and diagrams of troop movements differ somewhat from those of previous authors.

The most significant difference is in the location of the Sarcoxie road that approached Newtonia from the north, a road that the Federal troops used on September 30, 1862. Most previous maps have shown this road running due north out of Newtonia following the approximate route of present-day Teal Drive. It became clear to me, however, after reading every account of the battle that I could find (including after-action reports, newspaper reports, and postwar accounts), studying the lay of the land as it appears today, and taking into consideration certain other evidence, that the main Sarcoxie road ran northwest out of Newtonia, not due north, and that it did not approximate present-day Teal Drive.

Wiley Britton, who was a member of the Sixth Kansas Cavalry and who, after the war, wrote extensively about the first battle in *The Civil War on the Border* and *The Union Indian Brigade in the Civil War*, described the route of the Sarcoxie road followed by the Kansas troops in some detail, and he made it clear that the road, in its approach to Newtonia, came over the ridge northwest of town and entered the town through the lane formed by the stone walls just to the west of the Ritchey place. Why subsequent authors have not given more credence to Britton on this point is a minor mystery to me, particularly since Britton was from Newton County and presumably knew the area well.

In addition, when the bodies of some of the Union soldiers who had been buried at the cemetery north of Newtonia during the Civil War were dug up and reinterred in Springfield a few years after the war, the Sarcoxie road was used as a landmark to locate the graves, with each one designated as lying a certain number of feet *east* of the Sarcoxie road. It is clear from this evidence that the Sarcoxie road ran west of and adjacent to the cemetery. Thus, it becomes obvious why Colonel Cooper placed his artillery at the cemetery north of town during the First Battle of Newtonia. It was positioned there to guard the main approach to the town.

Several Union accounts of the First Battle of Newtonia mention the high ridge overlooking Newtonia that the troops came to as they drew within about a mile of the town. Today, the only ridge surrounding Newtonia that can be described as "high" and that is elevated enough to "overlook" the town lies to the west and northwest, not the north. Although the terrain of the area has undoubtedly changed somewhat since the time of the Civil War, the basic pattern of elevations has probably not changed markedly.

There may have been (and almost surely was) a fork of the Sarcoxie road that came into Newtonia about where Teal Drive enters the town today. Indeed, the map of the 1864 Newtonia battle from Cowles's *Official Military Atlas of the Civil War* shows two forks of the Sarcoxie road. However, both forks on this map approximate present-day Teal Drive. Either there was a third fork or one of the forks on the map is incorrectly positioned, because the route that was principally used by the Federal soldiers on September 30, 1862, ran near the cemetery and did not approximate Teal Drive.

A different understanding of where the Sarcoxie road ran necessarily alters one's understanding of troop movements as well. Most of the differences between my troop diagrams and those of previous authors can be accounted for by this altered conception of where the road was located. In at least one or two cases, however, the discrepancies have little, if anything, to do with where the road was located. For example, regardless of where the Sarcoxie road ran, a careful reading of the *Official Records* reveals that the action on the afternoon of September 30 between the Federal cavalry of Judson's

Sixth Kansas and the Confederate cavalry of Jeans and Stevens took place west of the Ritchey home, not east as some previous accounts have asserted.

The location of Camp Coffee at Big Springs has also been a subject of some debate. After-action accounts of the First Battle of Newtonia are not altogether clear on this point; however, the 1882 plat map of Newton County is. Big Springs, or Big Spring, was not just a temporary name that the Confederates gave their camp. It was the actual name of the place, and the 1882 map clearly shows that Big Springs was located about six miles southeast of Newtonia or about two miles west of present-day Fairview.

Present-day Shannon Springs, about three miles south of Newtonia, has been suggested by some as the possible site of Camp Coffee, but this does not seem likely. One can infer from Colonel Cooper's report of the Confederate evacuation of Newtonia that Camp Coffee lay some distance east of the Pineville road, not on the Pineville road. Also, Colonel Alexander's report of the first battle seems to imply that Camp Coffee was some considerable distance from Newtonia, not just a matter of two or three miles.

My only observation about troop movements during the Second Battle of Newtonia is that there is a tendency (at least I had such a tendency at one time) to assume that, since the Confederates were retreating southward and the battle was fought primarily from north and south, the Federals were pursuing from the north. In fact, of course, they were pursuing along the Granby road, which ran out of Newtonia more to the west than the north. When the Federals reached the ridge west of Newtonia on the Granby road and spotted the Confederate camps at the edge of the Indian Creek timber south of town near the Pineville road, the two sides were facing each other, as Cowles's atlas shows, from southeast to northwest. The Federals formed a battle line and left the road, flanking to the right with the town on their left, and advanced across the prairie in a southeasterly direction to meet the Confederates. Only after both sides formed behind east–west fences enclosing a field south of town did they face each other from north and south.

Bibliography

BOOKS AND MAGAZINES

Bearss, Edwin C. "The Army of the Frontier's First Campaign: The Confederates Win at Newtonia." *Missouri Historical Review* 60, no. 3 (April 1966): 283–319.

Britton, Wiley. *The Civil War on the Border*. 2 vols. New York: G.P. Putnam's Sons, 1899.

———. *The Union Indian Brigade in the Civil War*. Kansas City, MO: Franklin Hudson Publishing Co., 1922.

Burke, W.S. *Official Military History of Kansas Regiments During the War for the Suppression of the Great Rebellion*. 1870. Reprint, Ottawa: Kansas Heritage Press, n.d.

Cowles, Calvin D., comp. *The Official Military Atlas of the Civil War*. 1891. Reprint, New York: Arno Press, 1978.

Edwards, John N. *Shelby and His Men*. Cincinnati, OH: Miami Printing and Publishing Co., 1867.

Franks, Kenny A. *Stand Watie and the Agony of the Cherokee Nation*. Memphis, TN: Memphis State University Press, 1979.

Fryman, Robert J. *Engaged the Enemy Again: An Assessment of the 1862 and 1864 Civil War Battlefields at Newtonia, Missouri.* Atlanta, GA: Garrow & Associates, Inc., 1995.

Gaines, W. Craig. *The Confederate Cherokees: John Drew's Regiment of Mounted Rifles.* Baton Rouge: Louisiana State University Press, 1989.

Gass, W.T. "Two 'Close Calls.'" *Confederate Veteran* 12 (1904): 38–39.

Hinton, Richard Josiah. *Rebel Invasion of Missouri and Kansas, and the Campaign of the Army of the Border Against General Sterling Price in October and November, 1864.* Chicago: Church & Goodman, 1865.

History of Newton, Lawrence, Barry and McDonald Counties, Missouri. Pt. 1. Chicago: Goodspeed Publishing Co., 1888.

James, Larry A. *Newtonia the Prairie City.* Newtonia, MO: Newtonia Battlefields Protection Association, 2005.

Jobe, Sybil Shipley. *A History of Newton County Missouri as Portrayed in the Courthouse Mural.* Cassville, MO: Litho Printers, 1998.

Knight, Wilfred. *Red Fox: Stand Watie and the Confederate Indian Nations during the Civil War Years in Indian Territory.* Glendale, CA: Arthur H. Clark Company, 1988.

Laurance, G.W., comp. *A Biography of Judge M.H. Ritchey.* Edited by Larry A. James. Newtonia, MO: Newtonia Battlefields Protection Association, 2002.

McPheeters, William M. *I Acted from Principles: The Civil War Diary of Dr. William M. McPheeters, Confederate Surgeon in the Trans Mississippi.* Edited by Cynthia Dehaven Pitcock and Bill J. Gurley. Fayetteville: University of Arkansas Press, 2002.

Newtonia Battlefields Archaeological Survey. Mount Pleasant, TN: White Star Consulting, prepared for the Newtonia Battlefields Protection Association in cooperation with the Battlefield Protection Program of the National Park Service, 1998.

Norton, Richard L., ed. *Behind Enemy Lines: The Memoirs and Writings of Brigadier-General Sidney Drake Jackman.* Springfield, MO: Oak Hills Publishing, 1997.

Phillips, Christopher. *Missouri's Confederate: Claiborne Fox Jackson and the Creation of Southern Identity in the Border West.* Columbia: University of Missouri Press, 2000.

A Preservation Plan for the Civil War Battlefields of Newtonia, Missouri. Cincinnati, OH: Gray & Pape, Inc., prepared for the Newtonia Battlefields Protection Association, 2000.

Violette, Eugene Morrow. *A History of Missouri.* 1918. Reprint, Cape Girardeau, MO: Ramfre Press, 1960.

White, Christine Schultz, and Benton R. White. *Now the Wolf Has Come: The Creek Nation in the Civil War.* College Station: Texas A&M University Press, 1996.

Wood, Larry E. *The Civil War on the Lower Kansas-Missouri Border.* 2nd ed. Joplin, MO: Hickory Press, 2003.

ONLINE SOURCES

"Arizard-L Archives." Ancestry.com. http://listsearches.rootsweb.com.th/read/ARIZARD/1999-11/0943008441.

Encyclopedia of Oklahoma History and Culture, s.v. "Indian Expedition of 1862." Oklahoma Historical Society. http://digital.library.okstate.edu/encyclopedia/entries/I/IN009.html.

Meserve, John Bartlett. "Chief Opothleyahola." *Chronicles of Oklahoma* 9, no. 4 (December 1931). Available at http://digital.library.okstate.edu/chronicles/v009/v009p439.html.

Richardson, Albert D. *Beyond the Mississippi: From the Great River to the Great Ocean, Life and Adventures of the Prairies, Mountains and Pacific Coast.* Excerpt online at http://freepages.history.rootsweb.ancestry.com/~cappscreek/richardson.html.

Ridgely, F.M. Letter to Blow and Kennett of St. Louis, July 10, 1862. Blow Family Papers. Missouri Historical Society, St. Louis. Available at http://freepages.history.rootsweb.ancestry.com/~cappscreek/civilwar/or/granby1862.html.

UNPUBLISHED MANUSCRIPTS AND GOVERNMENT DOCUMENTS

Brown, John D. Letter, October 3, 1862. Tallman-Brown families, letters, 1861–1868. Western Historical Manuscript Collection, University of Missouri–Rolla.

Grabill, Mary. Letter entitled "To My Daughters." Transcribed copy on file at Wilson's Creek Battlefield National Park Library, Republic, Missouri.

James, Andrew Jackson. "History of Company M, Sixth Missouri State Militia Cavalry." Western Historical Manuscript Collection, University of Missouri–Columbia.

Murray, Thomas. Letter, October 8, 1862. Thomas Murray Correspondence, 1862–1867. Western Historical Manuscript Collection, University of Missouri–Rolla.

Rockwell, Jacob Harris. "A Rambling Reminiscence of Experiences During the Great War Between the States." Missouri Collection. Western Historical Manuscript Collection, University of Missouri–Columbia.

Thompson, M. Jeff. Memoirs. Western Historical Manuscript Collection, University of Missouri–Columbia.

U.S. Census, 1860, Newton County, Missouri. Microfilm copy at Joplin Public Library, Joplin, Missouri.

War of the Rebellion: A Compilation of Official Records of the Union and Confederate Armies. 1880–1902. Reprint, CD-ROM, Oakman, AL: H-Bar Enterprises, 1996.

NEWSPAPERS

Columbia Missouri Statesman, August 23, 1861.

Jefferson City Examiner, October 11, 1862.

Leavenworth Daily Conservative

Leavenworth Daily Times

Liberty Tribune, November 11, 1864.

St. Louis Tri-Weekly Missouri Republican, June 15, 1863.

Springfield Missouri Patriot. "Honor to Whom Honor Is Due." August 24, 1865. Transcribed copy of article at Wilson's Creek National Battlefield Library.

Wallace, Oliver V., ed. *Soldier's Letter, Second Colorado Cavalry: A Regimental Paper to Accompany the Regiment*. August 1864–November 28, 1865, nos. 31–37.

About the Author

L arry Wood is a retired public school teacher and freelance writer specializing in the history of the Ozarks region. His magazine articles have appeared in publications like *America's Civil War, Blue and Gray, Gateway Heritage, History Magazine, Kansas Heritage, Missouri Historical Review, Missouri Life, Ozarks Mountaineer, Ozarks Reader, Show Me the Ozarks, True West,* and *Wild West.* His previous books include *The Civil War on the Lower Kansas-Missouri Border, The Civil War Story of Bloody Bill Anderson, Other Noted Guerrillas of the Civil War in Missouri, Ozarks Gunfights and Other Notorious Incidents,* and two historical novels entitled *Call Me Charlie: A Novel of a Quantrill Raider* and *Showdown at Baxter Springs.* Wood and his wife, G.G., live in Joplin, Missouri.